Everything Good and Beautiful

Everything Good and Beautiful

A Devotional

SHAREEN ORCHARD

XULON PRESS

Xulon Press
2301 Lucien Way #415
Maitland, FL 32751
407.339.4217
www.xulonpress.com

Paperback ISBN-13: 978-1-66285-767-6
Ebook ISBN-13: 978-1-66285-768-3

Acknowledgements:

This project was birthed out of a time in my life that was full of business and a work-centered mindset. I was living in total event-planning mode and was not focusing on the Lord for His help! I am so thankful to serve with my boss, Taun Cortado, who does not hesitate to push me to God's Word in times where I need my stress relieved. He acknowledged my passion for writing and God's Word. Without his encouragement to get writing – this devotional would have never been started.

As my vision changed, I am thankful for the time my sister, Danielle Walker, spent to help me transcribe hundreds of sticky notes throughout the books of Genesis to Job so that more devotional days could be compiled.

Without my sweet friend, Hannah Loghry, continued transcription work and editing of many of these devotions would not have been possible. The Lord has placed the Loghry family in my life. Each of their four girls have made a deepening impact on my life as they have helped me in both my personal life and work life. It is so refreshing to experience the real-time work of God in Hannah as she helped me transcribe and edit. It is truly the Lord's leading through the words of this devotional.

Through the Writer's training with John Fornof, much character development was inspired. He taught me how to draw out different aspects of a situation or a given person. He helped me through times of writer's block and the fear of a blank page.

Although I learned important technical writing skills that have made this devotional what it is today, I will continually carry the joy-filled encouragement of my friend, John. Thanks for the training and being a "cheerleader" for me when I was stuck!

To my gifted Graphic Designer, Sydney Moon. You have grown into a beautiful young woman who is able to take a verbal description and create a masterpiece. The cover of this book is all that and more than what I would have ever imagined. You have done a beautiful and intimate job depicting the foundation and root of a growing treang tree which represents what I hope my readers will become as they read through these devotionals. Thank you to my niece!

I want to also thank my mother, Judy Orchard, for the countless hours she has spent editing hundreds of these days, and also doing a complete read-through to make certain my grammar was consistent. She and my Dad have stood behind me in supporting all that I do. They have prayed and encouraged me through life's tough moments. They trusted the Lord and stepped out in faith to adopt me all those years ago. Thank you for always trusting the Lord for your children no matter what we are facing in life.

My Grandma, Sally Ruff. There are not quite substantial words for the many unknown hours she spent before the Lord in prayer for me as I wrote each devotional day. Many of the bible sticky notes that these devotionals were transcribed from, come from the year and a half that I had the privilege to do care-giving for my precious Granddad, Dane Ruff. In those 18 months, I had the freedom to spend several hours with the Lord, but also see the strengthening faith of my Grandma and Grandad as they faithfully

Acknowledgements:

loved one another, prayed together, and served each other. That is a time in my life that I wouldn't change for the world. Thank you to my Grandma for carrying on the faithful legacy of Granddad, but also consistently persisting in prayer for this project.

DEDICATION

First and foremost, to my Grandma Sally, your prayers carried me through the writing of this devotional. You rejoiced with me as the Lord worked, and hit your knees in prayer when things were slow-moving. As Granddad always told me, before you all would pray for me, "The best place to be is in the center of God's will." This devotional has been just that. You have continued Granddad's legacy of praying for your grandkids and, for that, I will be forever grateful!

To Taun, you have never stopped pushing me to the Word of God. Without your question of, "What is God telling you?" and the countless times you watched my countenance change as I jumped into scripture — this devotional would not have been possible.

INTRODUCTION

For most people, this title, "Everything Good and Beautiful", seems a rather plain title. When we are young, we are told, "Don't judge a book by its cover."

My name, "Shareen", was given to me when I was adopted from India at six months old. "Shareen" means "Everything Good and Beautiful". Due to being malnourished when I was born, I had a lack of Vitamin A. This vitamin deficiency resulted in my diagnosis of Night Blindness at the age of five. With this disability, I have faced many challenges, and yet, I have seen God do incredible things with my life. My disability is a blessing, not a curse!

As I was thinking about a title for this devotional, these words, "Everything Good and Beautiful", seemed so fitting for how I, throughout my life, have learned to see scripture.

When I first began to write this devotional, it was simply something I thought I would pick up as a hobby because I love God's Word and through the years, He has taught me so much as I faced different challenges. Writing became a way to relieve my stress and I was getting into the Word. I wasn't really sure who I was writing it for at first — I just knew I needed to get all the lessons the Lord was teaching me down on paper!

Soon, as I told people what I was doing, writing this devotional became a project. One of my leaders asked if I was writing it with the intention of publishing it, and I just laughed. I never really thought about that aspect. Let alone that anyone would want to read my thoughts, from my times with the Lord. Boy was I wrong!!!

I originally geared this towards the women in my family — my Mom, Grandma, Aunts, Sisters, Nieces, and Cousins. But, I think that men would get a lot out of it too! We all have emotions and are called to function in life by standing on the Word of God — so, by all means, I pray that these daily devotionals will stir the hearts of many — men and women, both!

All scriptures are taken from www.biblegateway.com <http://www.biblegateway.com> ; Translation: NIV.

DAY 1

Acts 15:7

7 After much discussion, Peter got up and
addressed them: "Brothers, you know that some
time ago God made a choice among you that the
Gentiles might hear from my lips the message of
the gospel and believe.

Allow these verses to sink in, to wash over you with the depth
of God's love. As I read these verses, I am overwhelmed.
There are so many beautiful pieces to this passage. Peter takes a
stand and speaks truth that is so plain and yet, so rich. He directs
their thoughts back to God's actions. He says, "God made a choice
among you..." It wasn't that God was far off and distant. No. God
was among the people. How often do we get stuck in the past, for-
getting that God is among us? He wants to take his gospel forth
through us. Do we allow God to use us?

Day 2

Acts 15:8-9

8 God, who knows the heart, showed that he accepted them by giving the Holy Spirit to them just as he did to us. 9 He did not discriminate between us and them, for he purified their hearts by faith.

God knows our hearts and yet, he still chose to purify our hearts, by faith. When you are having a good day, rejoice that God chose to purify your heart. When you are having a bad day or those emotions are high and every irrational thought is coming to mind, rejoice that God has chosen to purify your heart – by faith! He purified your heart in advance. God accepted the Gentiles by giving them the Holy Spirit. He has done the same for us! Ask the Lord to help you walk in that.

Day 3

Acts 15:10-11

10 Now then, why do you try to test God by putting on the necks of Gentiles a yoke that neither we nor our ancestors have been able to bear? 11 No! We believe it is through the grace of our Lord Jesus that we are saved, just as they are."

The power of influence. It is so good to speak from our past because the Lord puts circumstances in our lives from which we are to mature and grow. But, are we choosing to influence others with the "law" of our past or are we speaking into their lives so that they might grow more in the Lord?

I love writing documentation! It's one of the favorite aspects of my job. I love to develop a process and then write the "How to" functionality so that others can learn from me. Although, I love writing documentation...it is easy for me to get stuck in the "law" of the process. I can place a yoke on someone as I teach them and I end up losing sight of the fact that I am able to write documentation so well because it is the gifting of the Lord in me.

It is through the grace of our Lord Jesus that we are able to influence others for the Kingdom because He is the one who has saved us and gifted us.

DAY 4

Romans 1:11-12

11 I long to see you so that I may impart to you
some spiritual gift to make you strong—12 that
is, that you and I may be mutually encouraged
by each other's faith.

These verses are so full of power! We, as women, have so much
to offer one another — no matter our age. The Lord has given
each of us a story that he is continually writing. These are stories
of spiritual gifts that he has imparted to us, so that we might make
one another strong! How are you allowing the Gospel to go forth
from your life to impart to others around you the spiritual gifts
God has entrusted to you? What testimony can you give so that
you and others may be mutually encouraged by each other's faith?

DAY 5

Lamentations 3:24

24 I say to myself, "The Lord is my portion; therefore, I will wait for him."

What are you facing today? Is it something that brings you joy? Or maybe something frustrating? Sorrowful? Worshipful? Whatever you are facing today, keep in mind that the Lord is your portion. Remembering this promise of God helps no matter what you are going through. If you are joyful because something great happened; or if you are full of sorrow or frustration because of tough times — the Lord is your portion.

As I have faced different circumstances in my life, the Lord is teaching me to say, "I am really angry about this…but the Lord is my portion." Or, "The Lord is my portion through these tears." Or, "I feel like I am being treated unfairly. The Lord is still my portion." This promise works both ways no matter what emotion or circumstance I am in. He is my portion therefore, I will wait on Him. Because He is my portion, I GET to wait on Him to move!!! Walking through life with this mindset makes a world of difference!

Day 6

Psalm 94:16-18

16 Who will rise up for me against the wicked?
Who will take a stand for me against evildoers?
17 Unless the Lord had given me help, I would
soon have dwelt in the silence of death. 18 When
I said, "My foot is slipping," your unfailing love,
Lord, supported me.

I love that the Psalmist was bold enough to ask such a question as, "Who will rise up for me against the wicked?" There is so much evil in this world and so many negative circumstances in our lives, that we begin to question if there is anyone who will stand up for us. Have you ever felt this way? You are so deep in the mud and your foot is slipping and you just feel so alone because the enemy's voice is so loud with lies?

Rest in the Lord! The Lord's UNFAILING love will support you. We, as believers — who have been chosen by our Heavenly Daddy, get to call upon Him when our foot is slipping and trust that his unfailing love will support us.

DAY 7

Psalm 94:19

19 When anxiety was great within me, your consolation brought me joy.

His joy consoles me in the midst of anxiety!!! Anxiety can be so overpowering in the moment and it makes you feel out of control. His word says that His joy is our consolation, our strength. He is our peace that surpasses all understanding! I praise God that He has placed simple promises in His Word that we can hold on to. Let his joy console you each and every day!

Day 8

Psalm 94:20-23

20 Can a corrupt throne be allied with you— a throne that brings on misery by its decrees? 21 The wicked band together against the righteous and condemn the innocent to death. 22 But the Lord has become my fortress, and my God the rock in whom I take refuge. 23 He will repay them for their sins and destroy them for their wickedness; the Lord our God will destroy them.

More and more, we see the wicked band together in an attempt to destroy the body of Christ. The enemy is very present against the righteous. This has gone on throughout history. We can continue to pray that the gospel will go forth as the Lord leads. The enemy is at work to bring disunity within the body of Christ, but the Lord has become our fortress. Will we go forward and battle with that mindset that God is our fortress?

When I think about God being my fortress and my rock in whom I take refuge, it makes it easier to pray for the wicked. Knowing that God is on my side, fills me with love and the reminder that each of us stands before the Lord and gives account for our own actions. So how will we act today? Hmm…not sure I like that question.

DAY 9

Luke 22:31-32

31 "Simon, Simon, Satan has asked to sift all
of you as wheat. 32 But I have prayed for you,
Simon, that your faith may not fail. And when
you have turned back, strengthen your brothers."

Jesus called Simon by name. In these two short verses, Jesus says
Simon's name three different times. Jesus lets Simon know of
Satan's intentions to sift each of us like wheat. How many times
throughout the Word of God, do we hear of Satan's plans? But,
Jesus — the Son of God — is interceding for us.

He says, "Hey! Satan has asked to sift you like wheat. He wants
to take you out. But I AM PRAYING FOR YOU. I, the God of
the Universe, Your Abba, Daddy, Father. My child — whom I call
my own — I am praying for you. And here is what I am specifically
praying for you: That your faith may not fail." Our Daddy knows
we are going to fall short. He knows we will fail. But I love his call
to action in verse 32, "And when you have turned back, strengthen
your brothers." This tells me to give testimony of God's faithfulness
as I face trials, and encourage others with what the Lord has done.

Day 10

1 Corinthians 12:21
21 The eye cannot say to the hand, "I don't need you!" And the head cannot say to the feet, "I don't need you!"

How many times have you faced a situation, good or bad, and said, "I don't want to burden anyone with my problems"? And so, you don't ask for help. God created unity and community for a reason, but we live in such an individualistic society, that we figure we can do things on our own. We think others are too busy to help us.

This verse overflows with the need for one another, in the body of Christ. How do we make our needs known in such a way that allows others to be a blessing to us? Because of my disability, I struggle with that mindset. I don't want to burden others, but I have found that if I don't let people know my needs, I will miss out on building a lot of great relationships. Therefore I am learning to lean on others.

DAY 11

Jonah 4:4

4 But the Lord replied, "Is it right for you to be angry?"

How intimate is our God that he would put this question in his Word? And make it a stand-alone verse? When this question is coming from the Lord Almighty, it becomes very sobering and a great way to get our minds back on the Lord and his ways. If we are following the Lord, do we really have a reason to have any negative emotions? But that is our flesh.

So, when you are angry about a big issue or maybe just because you stubbed your toe — just remember this question. Lord willing, it will put a smile on your face and joy in your heart. I don't know about you, but whenever I read this verse, I can't help but chuckle and say, "Okay Lord. I got your point."

Day 12

Deuteronomy 8:2-3

2 Remember how the Lord your God led you all the way in the wilderness these forty years, to humble and test you in order to know what was in your heart, whether or not you would keep his commands. 3 He humbled you, causing you to hunger and then feeding you with manna, which neither you nor your ancestors had known, to teach you that man does not live on bread alone but on every word that comes from the mouth of the Lord.

The Lord tests and humbles us in order to know what is in our hearts. He has a purpose for everything that we go through. Let us never forget that. If the Lord didn't bring circumstances in our lives, would we really know what is in our hearts and where we need to grow more in His likeness?

Are we living our lives on his Word alone? He allows us to go through circumstances in our lives, so that we hunger for Him and learn that we don't just live on bread alone, but on His Word. What a way to walk through this life. Allow the Lord to humble and test you, so that He may reveal to you what is in your heart. It may not be pretty, but He is faithful to not leave us where we are! So, rest in your Daddy's arms!

Day 13

Exodus 16:6-8

6 So Moses and Aaron said to all the Israelites, "In the evening you will know that it was the Lord who brought you out of Egypt, 7 and in the morning you will see the glory of the Lord, because he has heard your grumbling against him. Who are we, that you should grumble against us?" 8 Moses also said, "You will know that it was the Lord when he gives you meat to eat in the evening and all the bread you want in the morning, because he has heard your grumbling against him. Who are we? You are not grumbling against us, but against the Lord."

Depending on the stage of life in which we are, authorities in our lives may look different for each of us. Your authority, perhaps your Mom, Dad, Teacher, Grandma, Boss, Leader, Pastor, whoever it is, the Lord has placed that authority in your life. He puts these authorities over us, so that we can learn about Him through them.

I have had a number of authorities throughout my life. Some good. Some bad. Some are really in tune with the Spirit of God. And some, not so much. I have grumbled against a lot of them. I have complained and thought I knew better. I have told my authorities "no" and found that isn't always a good idea...at all. Then this passage of scripture was brought to my attention and the Lord used this to check my heart. I was reminded that when I grumble against my authorities, I am grumbling against the Lord Most High. I can only speak from my own experience, but I need this reminder every day.

Challenge, if you so desire to take it: Ask the Lord which authorities you have grumbled against in your life. Maybe it is someone from your past, but does the Lord want to heal that relationship or restore respect for that authority? If you step out in obedience to the Lord and that person doesn't respond as you think he or she should, remember he/she gives account to the Lord for his/her actions — just as you do. The Lord is faithful to show us where we need change and healing. He prompts us to let things go.

DAY 14

Exodus 20:18-20

18 When the people saw the thunder and lightning and heard the trumpet and saw the mountain in smoke, they trembled with fear. They stayed at a distance 19 and said to Moses, "Speak to us yourself and we will listen. But do not have God speak to us or we will die." 20 Moses said to the people, "Do not be afraid. God has come to test you, so that the fear of God will be with you to keep you from sinning."

We have two choices in life. We can run to man asking him to go to the Lord on our behalf. Or we can sit before the Lord — one on one — and be tested by Him so that we may grow in the fear of the Lord. Which person are you?

The Lord puts people in our lives that can counsel us and guide us through situations. But one of the most eye-opening things I have learned is that I tend to run to people, instead of going directly to the Lord. Oftentimes the Lord will speak through his people. Even as you read this daily devotional, I pray that He is using it in your life. More importantly, I pray that you will run to the Lord and learn to fear Him on your own. He longs to have a personal relationship with you every day, so get in the Word!

DAY 15

Genesis 37:4

4 When his brothers saw that their father loved him more than any of them, they hated him and could not speak a kind word to him.

It's amazing how quickly the thought of hatred can fill one's mind and build up walls. This verse is a great example. Have you ever been so consumed with hatred toward a sibling that you couldn't speak a kind word to him? Reading this verse makes me want to point fingers at Joseph's brothers and say, "Wow! They had some major family issues."

We each have family issues because no one is perfect, but how do we deal with them? If our family situations were to be written in the Bible, what would be written? Thinking this way really makes me point a finger back at myself and ask the Lord to help me check my heart. Where do I need to ask for forgiveness?

DAY 16

Genesis 37:5-10

5 Joseph had a dream, and when he told it to his brothers, they hated him all the more. 6 He said to them, "Listen to this dream I had: 7 We were binding sheaves of grain out in the field when suddenly my sheaf rose and stood upright, while your sheaves gathered around mine and bowed down to it." 8 His brothers said to him, "Do you intend to reign over us? Will you actually rule us?" And they hated him all the more because of his dream and what he had said. 9 Then he had another dream, and he told it to his brothers. "Listen," he said, "I had another dream, and this time the sun and moon and eleven stars were bowing down to me." 10 When he told his father as well as his brothers, his father rebuked him and said, "What is this dream you had? Will your mother and I and your brothers actually come and bow down to the ground before you?"

What powerful dreams Joseph had! I wonder if he went to his brothers with great pride in telling them his dream or did he go to them with humility? I would have loved to be a fly on the wall during this family conversation, to watch the dynamics of each one's personality. The response of hatred from Joseph's brothers is very clear throughout these verses. The more Joseph talked about his dreams, the more hatred they had for him. I can't say I would be thrilled if one of my sisters came to me and told me she had a dream that I was going to bow down to her. I would have probably laughed in her face!

The more I think about the context of Joseph's story, I wonder if he knew these dreams were from the Lord? Did he know he was speaking the plans of God? And as for his brothers' response, they weren't hating against Joseph alone. No, their hatred was towards the Lord.

When you have a dream or something the Lord puts in your Spirit, be bold and share it. It may sound super crazy, but share it with people you trust and see what the Lord does.

DAY 17

Genesis 37:11
11 His brothers were jealous of him, but his
father kept the matter in mind.

I love that his father questions Joseph's dream, but didn't fully dismiss it. This reminds me of how the LORD continually spoke to me about returning to Gospel for Asia ministry and I had to go to my dad and tell him I wasn't supposed to get a job. Okay, a bit of a different situation and there wasn't any sibling rivalry. But the fact is, that Joseph was bold enough to share his dreams, as crazy as they may have sounded to his family. My parents were faithful to pray about the realization of my dream no matter how crazy it may have sounded to them.

We don't get to choose what family we are a part of, but the Lord has blessed me with parents who believe the Lord on my behalf. Not every kid is that lucky. Believe that as you share your dreams with your parents or people you trust, that the Lord will bring them in line with that dream in time. He will give them the faith to trust Him. The Lord is good!

Day 18

Genesis 37:14

14 So he said to him, "Go and see if all is well
with your brothers and with the flocks, and bring
word back to me." Then he sent him off from the
Valley of Hebron…"

Although Joseph's father didn't know the future of his son's
plans — would his father have had guilt for sending Joseph
out to check on his brothers? Joseph — the son his father loved
the most. How does a parent process through a situation when
something terrible happens to their child?

I am not a parent, but as I read this verse, I think about our
Heavenly Father's relationship with his Son and how the Father
covered all sins and guilt and acts of the flesh by sending His Son
to the cross. There is redemption through Jesus's death on the cross.

So, no matter what decisions you make as a parent, they are
covered by the blood of Christ as you walk with Him. And for us,
as children, when we don't agree with something our parents do or
when we think we know better than they do, we can remember that
their actions are covered by the blood of Christ. So, we can entrust
our parents to the Lord just as they entrust each of us to the Lord!

DAY 19

Genesis 37:18

18 But they saw him in the distance, and before
he reached them, they plotted to kill him.

You know — I wouldn't want to give account for the act of
plotting to kill a sibling. But that gets me thinking of my
own thoughts for which I would not want to give account. Is that
enough to make me want to think differently? If my thoughts
about myself were more Christ centered, then I would be able to
see others through Christ. Having the mindset of Christ would
make each of us less fearful, anxious, and insecure.

What thoughts would you not want to account for when you
stand before the Lord?

DAY 20

Genesis 37:21-22

21 When Reuben heard this, he tried to rescue him from their hands. "Let's not take his life," he said. 22 "Don't shed any blood. Throw him into this cistern here in the wilderness, but don't lay a hand on him." Reuben said this to rescue him from them and take him back to his father.

You would have to have some major bitterness and anger in your heart to go through with the brothers' plan to kill Joseph. Talk about family dysfunction!

BUT then there is Rueben who desires to save his brother's life. It's a choice…good or bad? The LORD gives us the freedom to choose…whether we acknowledge Him or not. How do we glorify God through the freedom to choose that He gives us each and every day?

DAY 21

Psalm 150:2

2 Praise him for his acts of power; praise him for
his surpassing greatness.

This verse is a call to action. Something that we, as believers,
get to do each day! Praise Him — the Most High God, Abba,
Father. He is our shelter and strong tower. Praise him for his great
acts of power. Wow! What great acts of God's power do you see
in your life for which you can praise God?

Many times, my brain is often stuck on the here and now. I
focus on whatever is right in front of my face. Praise him for his
surpassing greatness! As you read that, doesn't that just delight
your heart? It really makes my day so much better!

Day 22

1 Samuel 3:7

7 Now Samuel did not yet know the Lord: The word of the Lord had not yet been revealed to him.

No wonder that Samuel did not know that it was the Lord who was speaking to him. It is so important for us to have a relationship with the Lord that is strengthened by being continuously in the Word. We can get so busy with life, but if we don't know the Lord personally, then we will miss out on His revelation of His Word.

Keep close to God through reading His Word. He is near and His timing is perfect in revealing himself to us. He is patient with us and will repeat himself until we hear, just as he did with Samuel.

DAY 23

1 Samuel 3:9

9 So Eli told Samuel, "Go and lie down, and if he calls you, say, 'Speak, Lord, for your servant is listening.'" So Samuel went and lay down in his place.

It is so important to have people in our lives who will point us to the Lord. Do you have an Eli in your life who will tell you to go back and listen for the Lord's voice?

"So Samuel went and lay down in his place." What a beautiful way to respond. There is such a strong sense of full obedience and respect for the authority that the Lord has placed in Samuel's life. For the authorities that the Lord has placed in your life, are you willing to listen and obey them? Yes–those authorities will disappoint you, but if you just look at them as someone who is above you — there will be failure. They are only human. I have found that it is a lot easier to trust man when I see it as trusting the LORD in them. The Lord will use them just as he used Eli in Samuel's life.

DAY 24

1 Samuel 3:10

10 The Lord came and stood there, calling as at the other times, "Samuel! Samuel!" Then Samuel said, "Speak, for your servant is listening."

The other three times the Lord called Samuel, it only says that "he called..." But the fourth time, it says the Lord came and stood there!!! Can you imagine having face-to-face time with the Lord? He is so patient with us and reveals himself to us in His perfect timing.

I pray, today, that we would not be so distracted by our daily tasks that we would miss the Lord standing before us.

Day 25

1 Samuel 3:14

14 Therefore I swore to the house of Eli, 'The guilt of Eli's house will never be atoned for by sacrifice or offering.'"

Wow! I can't imagine this wrath. This is the first time the Lord speaks to Samuel and this is what Samuel hears.

I don't know if I would want to have the Lord speak to me again, if this is what He said the first time His word was revealed to me.

Have you ever been in Samuel's position? Maybe it wasn't the first time the Lord had ever spoken to you, but are there times the Lord tells you something that you really didn't want to hear? What do you do with those words from the Lord? How do you process them or take ownership?

Day 26

1 Samuel 3:15

15 Samuel lay down until morning and then opened the doors of the house of the Lord. He was afraid to tell Eli the vision,

On day 25, we talked about 1 Samuel 3:14 and how there are times the Lord speaks words that we don't always want to hear. So, how did Samuel respond to this word from the Lord? He was afraid to share the vision with Eli.

How often have I had the confidence to share the things the Lord reveals to me? Keep in mind, if you have a word from the Lord, there is nothing to fear. When you are in the moment, it can be really hard to remember that — especially if it is a word of wrath, like it was with Samuel. Ask the Lord to check your heart and trust him to remove the fear and give you the confidence to speak the words that he has spoken to you.

Day 27

1 Samuel 3:18

18 So Samuel told him everything, hiding nothing from him. Then Eli said, "He is the Lord; let him do what is good in his eyes."

Talk about taking ownership of what the Lord speaks! We should not fear sharing with leaders, or people in authority, what the Lord is showing us. We should leave it to the Lord to do what is right in his eyes. As you share the words God has given you, you also must trust Him with whatever the response may be. Remember, we each stand before the Lord and give account for our own actions.

DAY 28

1 Samuel 3:19

19 The Lord was with Samuel as he grew up, and
he let none of Samuel's words fall to the ground

O h how beautiful! There is hope in the Lord! We can sit and
fear sharing with others, or we can choose to trust the Lord.
Just as He was with Samuel, we can have the confidence that He
will be with us.

There is an overwhelming feeling of the greatness of God as I
read the last part of this verse, "…and he let none of Samuel's words
fall to the ground." Wow! Praise the Lord! Don't be afraid to work
with the Lord through your fears about sharing with others what
He has told you. He is on your side. We have the privilege to pray
that the Lord would not let any of our words fall to the ground!

Day 29

1 Corinthians 1:18

18 For the message of the cross is foolishness to those who are perishing, but to us who are being saved it is the power of God.

This verse brings such simple truth to the forefront of my mind as I read it. It is a simple truth, yet it is so deep and challenging to my heart. Do I live my life as though the message of the cross is the power of God? Or do I live my life more as though the message of the cross is foolishness?

Do I only acknowledge the cross at Easter or when I am struggling through a problem? I can only point the finger at myself and question my actions. You know, I can be a good Christian and say all the right Bible verses — but I want my life to show the real power of God. I want to walk in the power of the cross and its healing embrace.

There is a worship song sung by Cody Carnes called, "The Cross Has the Final Word". The words are simple, yet so powerful.

"The cross has the final word.
The cross has the final word.
Sorrow may come in the darkest night.
The cross has the final word.
The cross has the final word.

The cross has the final word.
Evil may put up its strongest fight.
The cross has the final word.
The cross has the final word.
The cross has the final word.
The Savior has come with the morning light.
The cross has the final word.
The cross has the final word.
The cross has the final word.
He traded death for eternal life.
The cross has the final word.

I would like to challenge you to search your heart before the Lord and ask Him to show you how you can live your life as though the cross has the final word. And then go live that life! I can promise you that although you may fail, if you hold tight to the cross, its message will not be one of foolishness, but rather, the power of God! The cross truly has the final word. Period.

Day 30

1 Corinthians 1:25

25 For the foolishness of God is wiser than human wisdom, and the weakness of God is stronger than human strength.

This is just a great verse. Some verses just really speak for themselves and need to be left for reflection between you and the Lord.

Day 31

Colossians 1:22

22 But now he has reconciled you by Christ's physical body through death to present you holy in his sight, without blemish and free from accusation—

To be free from accusation. What does that mean? No one can accuse me, nor can I accuse myself. How very freeing! If you, as my brother or sister in Christ, are trusting in the salvation of God — that means I cannot accuse you.

Christ's death on the cross presents us as holy in his sight, without blemish. So let me ask you this: in all your fleshly imperfections, do you believe that He presents you holy in His sight, without blemish?

If we really cling to the promises of God — it changes everything.

Day 32

Matthew 27:52-53

52 and the tombs broke open. The bodies of many holy people who had died were raised to life. 53 They came out of the tombs after Jesus' resurrection and [a] went into the holy city and appeared to many people

Honestly at first read, these verses are a bit creepy. To think of dead people coming up out of the ground and going into the city to appear to many people. But the glory of God is so real in the rising up of the dead in this situation. These are people who have gone before us. Believers in the Lord who have stories to tell.

I wonder what these people said to those in the city?! Do we have the mind of eternity to rest in the Lord and what is to come?

Day 33

Jeremiah 31:35-37

35 This is what the Lord says, he who appoints the sun to shine by day, who decrees the moon and stars to shine by night, who stirs up the sea so that its waves roar— the Lord Almighty is his name: 36 "Only if these decrees vanish from my sight," declares the Lord, "will Israel ever cease being a nation before me." 37 This is what the Lord says: "Only if the heavens above can be measured and the foundations of the earth below be searched out will I reject all the descendants of Israel because of all they have done," declares the Lord.

Today, simply think upon who God is. He is the one who appoints the sun to shine. He decrees the moon and stars to shine by night. Let that sink in. Delight in the Lord.

"This is what the Lord says: 'Only if the heavens above can be measured and the foundations of the earth below be searched out will I reject all the descendants of Israel because of all they have done,' declares the Lord."

Deep breath. No matter what you have done — the Lord will not reject you! Rest in this promise!

DAY 34

1 Corinthians 15:58

58 Therefore, my dear brothers and sisters, stand firm. Let nothing move you. Always give yourselves fully to the work of the Lord, because you know that your labor in the Lord is not in vain.

If you are in ministry, or have been in ministry, or see your work place as your mission field — then this promise holds true for you. We have the confidence given to us, by the Lord, to stand firm in Him. The word says, "Let nothing move you".

What if, for today, you were to face a situation and say, "Let nothing move me"? What would the outcome be? It could be a personal problem. It could be a project that just isn't going right. Or maybe you have too many work issues on your plate right now. What about your kids or you dealing with your kids — did one of you wake up on the wrong side of the bed? "Let nothing move me."

Last but not least, we are called to always give ourselves fully to the work of the Lord. He put us on earth for a reason and the work that we do "in the Lord" is not in vain.

So, today as you actively repeat the words, "Let nothing move me," also remember to work as unto the Lord–fully, completely, giving your all. And if you don't feel like working as unto the Lord, ask the Lord for His help. He is faithful!

Day 35

Isaiah 30:18-19

18 Yet the Lord longs to be gracious to you; therefore he will rise up to show you compassion. For the Lord is a God of justice. Blessed are all who wait for him! 19 People of Zion, who live in Jerusalem, you will weep no more. How gracious he will be when you cry for help! As soon as he hears, he will answer you.

Our Daddy, our Abba Father, longs to be gracious to us! He will rise up to show compassion to us. Our God is a giving God. Later in the verse it says, "As soon as he hears, he will answer you." Our God wants to talk to us, to answer us as we cry out to Him. Thank you, Daddy!

DAY 36

Psalm 34:8-9

8 Taste and see that the Lord is good; blessed is the one who takes refuge in him. 9 Fear the Lord, you his holy people, for those who fear him lack nothing.

Have you ever thought about the intricacy of your taste buds? To think that the Lord created us to have taste buds so that we can determine what is good and what is bad. It's the same thing with the Lord's goodness. His word tells us to "taste and see that the Lord is good." Sometimes what we think is bad, is still good. When we have the Lord's perspective, even the worst of situations can be made good. We are blessed when we take refuge in the Lord. That isn't just some nice sentence in the Bible. There is so much blessing when we take refuge in the Lord.

So, if you taste and see that the Lord is good, you will be blessed as you take refuge in Him. As we take refuge in Him, we learn to fear Him. Fear the Lord and you will lack nothing. What if we were to walk that out in our daily lives? What would that look like or mean for you today to walk in the fear of the Lord, to take refuge in Him, and to taste and see that He is good?

Day 37

Psalm 27:1

1 The Lord is my light and my salvation— whom shall I fear? The Lord is the stronghold of my life— of whom shall I be afraid?

Dictionary.com <http://Dictionary.com> defines the word stronghold as, "A well-fortified place; fortress". The Lord is the stronghold, the fortress, of our lives. It is easy to read over these words and just pass them by. But, there are so many times that I have feared people or unknown circumstances and not faced them as though the Lord is my stronghold or my fortress.

If the Lord is my light, my salvation, and my stronghold, then I really have no reason to fear in life. Easier said than done. I want to encourage you to face your day today as though the Lord is your stronghold. I pray that the Lord will show you how to walk this verse out for today. Or maybe you are at a point where you just need to focus on asking the Lord to be your stronghold for whatever you face in the next hour. That is OK. The Lord is patient with us and will walk with us, hand in hand, moment by moment.

Day 38

Psalm 27:2

2 When the wicked advance against me to devour[a] me, it is my enemies and my foes who will stumble and fall.

This verse proves that our enemies are already defeated by the Lord! But, the problem is, we don't always live with such a victorious mindset. Instead, we live in fear. Well, maybe this is just my own issue. But, if you struggle with living as though God already has defeated our enemies and that they are the ones who will stumble and fall — I would encourage you to hold tightly to this particular verse. Let it sink into every fiber of your being, then sit back and watch what the Lord Almighty will do!

DAY 39

Psalm 27:3

3 Though an army besiege me, my heart will not fear; though war break out against me, even then I will be confident.

Oh how wonderful to have a heart that doesn't fear. I love this verse, because even in reading it, I am filled with confidence from the Lord. There is such a sigh of relief and peace to be had in this verse.

Even though there is an army and war is breaking out against me, his Word says that I can be confident. No matter what is going on. No matter whether it is a war in your home or at work. No matter whether it is a mental war or even something you are battling with the Lord — even then we can be confident that the Lord is going to bring relief. Don't give up! Stick it out and ask Him to give you the confidence you need in the midst of the armies and war.

Day 40

Psalm 27:4-5

4 One thing I ask from the Lord, this only do I seek: that I may dwell in the house of the Lord all the days of my life, to gaze on the beauty of the Lord and to seek him in his temple. 5 For in the day of trouble he will keep me safe in his dwelling; he will hide me in the shelter of his sacred tent and set me high upon a rock.

Verse 4 is great because it shows how David is seeking the Lord to get to that place of dwelling with Him. But then comes verse 5, which tells us what the Lord will do for His children as they dwell in Him. This is the God that we serve— "For in the day of trouble he will keep me safe in his dwelling; he will hide me in the shelter of his sacred tent and set me high upon a rock." I would have to say that this is a good deal.

So, remember these three things as you dwell in the Lord:

1. In the day of trouble He will keep you safe.
2. He will hide you in the shelter of his sacred tent.
3. He will set you high upon a rock.

Take time to dwell in Him today, whatever that may look like for you. He is waiting with open arms to hide you in safety and pick you up to put you high upon a rock!

Day 41

Psalm 27:6-7

6 Then my head will be exalted above the enemies who surround me; at his sacred tent I will
sacrifice with shouts of joy; I will sing and make
music to the Lord. 7 Hear my voice when I call,
Lord; be merciful to me and answer me.

This shall be our response to His protection. We learned on day 40 that He will hide us and place us on a high rock. As we experience these things, we can respond with sacrifices of praise and singing to the Lord.

How great is it that the Lord gives us step by step directions through His Word? He doesn't just tell us he is going to keep us safe, shelter us, and place us on a high rock. I mean, it is great that he is going to do all these things — as well as exalt our head above our enemies — but, what are we to do once we are in the place?

Praise the Lord that he doesn't call us to sit in silence. He doesn't move us into a shelter so we can sit like a bump on a log! We get to sacrifice with shouts of joy!!! We get to sing and make music! We get to be loud! :) So be loud today and praise him as you sit in his shelter!!!

Day 42

Psalm 27:8
8 My heart says of you, "Seek his face!" Your face,
Lord, I will seek.

Are there days that you talk to the Lord and wonder if he is
even listening? I love that the Psalmist wasn't afraid to be
direct with the Lord. He says, "Hear my voice when I call, Lord".
He asks Him to be merciful and answer when he calls. We can do
the same thing with the Lord. As we cry out to the Lord, we can
ask Him to listen and answer.

I was praying through some things one night and asking the
Lord for direction. I really was wrestling with finding the right
answer and solution to the problem. But, then I heard that still
small voice, "Shareen — get in my Word. The answer is in my
Word. Romans 1." Well, duh! I read Romans 1 and saw the Lord
lead me to the exact answer that I was needing.

"My heart says of you, 'Seek his face!' Your face, Lord, I will
seek." As you seek the Lord, be willing to listen to your heart and
the Holy Spirit — in them you will find the right direction. Just as
I heard the Lord tell me to get into His Word, that was my heart
telling me to "Seek his face!"

DAY 43

Psalm 27:9

9 Do not hide your face from me, do not turn your servant away in anger; you have been my helper. Do not reject me or forsake me, God my Savior.

Over the last few days, we have seen how the Lord is lifting up our head and protecting us from our enemies. Praise the Lord! Then you get to Psalm 27:9 and the Psalmist is crying out to the Lord saying, "Don't turn away from me. Don't forget me. Don't turn me away in anger. Lord, you have been by my side. Please don't reject me or forsake me." (Paraphrase mine.)

Although things can be going well, there are those days that we just hit rough patches and feel like we are falling apart. As we read this verse, I think it is good to take heart and see that the Psalmist was bold in crying out to the Lord asking Him not to forget His child. Always remember where the Lord has brought you from and in that, ask him not to forget you. He is your God and your Savior.

DAY 44

Psalm 27:10-12

10 Though my father and mother forsake me,
the Lord will receive me. 11 Teach me your way,
Lord; lead me in a straight path because of my
oppressors. 12 Do not turn me over to the desire
of my foes, for false witnesses rise up against me,
spouting malicious accusations.

This passage truly describes what often happens in the lives of
our brothers and sisters who are taking the gospel to those
who have yet to hear of Jesus. Our brothers and sisters are dis-
owned by their father and mother, they are led on crooked paths
by their oppressors, and false witnesses speak maliciously against
them. Sharing the gospel in a nation where Christianity is not the
prominent religion is one of the most difficult tasks.

I would encourage you to take time today and pray for our
brothers and sisters who are serving in this way. Pray that they
would take ownership of the promise that, even though their father
and mother may disown them, the Lord will be there to receive
them. Ask the Lord to direct their paths and help them love those
who are maliciously accusing them.

He is faithful!

Day 45

Psalm 27:13

13 I remain confident of this: I will see the goodness of the Lord in the land of the living.

What a great promise to pray over those believers or
non-believers with whom you come in contact. We can
be confident that no matter what we are going through, we will see
the goodness of the Lord. Then we can take this a step further and
believe this promise on behalf of others. The goodness of the Lord
is always present. That doesn't mean it is always easy to see, but
we can ask the Lord to make us confident in seeing HIs goodness!

DAY 46

Psalm 27:14
14 Wait for the Lord; be strong and take heart
and wait for the Lord.

This seems like a simple command for us to follow. Wait on the Lord. Be strong and take heart. This may be one of the commands in the Bible that could be easier said than done. But, if we were to actually live this verse out for today and go step by step — it is doable. The great thing is, as you wait on the LORD — you can ask Him to help you wait on Him.

I pray that you will be able to wait on the Lord in all you do today. In this, I know you will be able to be strong and take heart, for you will find his many blessings.

DAY 47

Genesis 13:17

17 Go, walk through the length and breadth of
the land, for I am giving it to you."

As I read this verse, I know that it is referring to walking
around an actual piece of land that the Lord is giving to
his servant. But, I got to thinking, "land" in my own life has never
meant an actual piece of land. I can see how I can still apply this
verse. This verse is about taking ownership and believing the Lord
for the things that he is giving you.

Maybe that "land" in your life is a relationship or a job or a
home for your family. Whatever it is, are you ready to walk? Can
you trust the Lord to give you the land? Even more so, are you
willing to walk all the steps out to take the land? Sometimes that
is the hardest part.

Day 48

Leviticus 19:14

14 "'Do not curse the deaf or put a stumbling block in front of the blind, but fear your God. I am the Lord.

There truly is a verse in the Bible for even those who have a disability! This verse shows the compassion and kindness of the Lord because he has even taken the time to tell people what NOT to do to the deaf and blind. What a beautiful thing! The opposite of cursing the deaf and putting a stumbling block in front of the blind is to FEAR THE LORD.

We are called to fear the Lord instead of making fun of the disabled. How great is it that we are to put our energy towards fearing the Lord. It changes your mindset doesn't it? As one who is legally blind and has had "stumbling blocks" put in front of her by others, I would challenge you to ask the Lord to help you fear Him and I hope that as you fear Him, you will begin to see Him guide you in wisdom to understand the person who is deaf or blind. You may just be amazed how blessed you will be in the end.

DAY 49

Leviticus 19:23-25

23 "'When you enter the land and plant any kind of fruit tree, regard its fruit as forbidden.[a] For three years you are to consider it forbidden[b]; it must not be eaten. 24 In the fourth year all its fruit will be holy, an offering of praise to the Lord. 25 But in the fifth year you may eat its fruit. In this way your harvest will be increased. I am the Lord your God.

Who needs a "how to" manual when you can just read the Bible? We are given instructions about planting trees. If you have ever planted fruit trees, you will have seen this passage of scripture come to life. The process of planting any kind of tree is hard work and can be frustrating at times.

I think about all the hard work and love that has been put into the fruit trees and perimeter trees on the Gospel for Asia campus. The process of planting trees and tying them to keep them straight was arduous. But now, years later, we are seeing the growth right before our eyes!

Be patient with the growing process — whether that be in your life or in the life of a tree. You will bear much fruit over time. Be sure to follow His instructions through His Word. Remember, He is the Lord your God!

Day 50

Ruth 4:7-8

7 (Now in earlier times in Israel, for the redemption and transfer of property to become final, one party took off his sandal and gave it to the other. This was the method of legalizing transactions in Israel.) 8 So the guardian-redeemer said to Boaz, "Buy it yourself." And he removed his sandal.

Interesting how the Israelites removed a sandal in order to confirm a transaction. It is good to learn about different traditions. I think about the people in South Asia and how they will remove their sandals before entering a church building or temple. We participate in many cultural traditions of which we probably don't even think twice about their purpose or meaning.

Day 51

2 Kings 12:15
15 They did not require an accounting from those
to whom they gave the money to pay the workers,
because they acted with complete honesty.

We are called to give the first fruits of our finances back to the work of the Lord, but how do you choose the ministry or the church to which you give? Obviously, we have financial guidelines set in place for our personal finances and expectations of accountability for those to whom we give. And we trust the Lord to guide us in the choices we make.

No church or organization is perfect. Every man will make a mistake because we live in a fallen world. Who do you listen to as you consider where to invest your money in furthering God's kingdom? I pray and challenge you to listen to the Lord and ask him to reveal to you the integrity of the church or organization to which you choose to give. However, our first fruits are to be given to the Lord, not man. We are to give with a cheerful heart!

Day 52

1 Chronicles 5:20

20 They were helped in fighting them, and God delivered the Hagrites and all their allies into their hands, because they cried out to him during the battle. He answered their prayers, because they trusted in him.

What an awesome reminder that we need to call out to God in the midst of the battle and believe that He will answer our prayers. The Lord will answer as we trust Him! It is not just a matter of talking to the Lord when things are going well and life is great. No, we must cry out to Him in the midst of the battle — beginning, middle, and end.

We can't just say some words and end with an "amen". We need to believe the Lord for what we are asking and trust that He will answer. We have been given faith for a reason!

DAY 53

1 Chronicles 17:13-14

13 I will be his father, and he will be my son. I will never take my love away from him, as I took it away from your predecessor. 14 I will set him over my house and my kingdom forever; his throne will be established forever.'"

This is the hope that we have in Jesus! His throne will be established forever. It is eternal. Everything about the Son of Man is eternal. The Lord says that he will never take his love away from his Son. Point taken. Praise the Lord!

Day 54

1 Chronicles 17:25

25 "You, my God, have revealed to your servant that you will build a house for him. So your servant has found courage to pray to you.

One day, the Lord put on my heart to begin praying for the home I would have with my future spouse. I was asking the Lord, "How do I pray for that?" He encouraged me to pray for a solid structure. A home that would be filled with peace and hospitality. I felt so joyful as the Lord walked me through how to pray for my future home.

Little did I know, that when I was picking verses for this devotional a few days prior, that this verse would be so real and evident in the midst of what I was praying for! When I was reading back through the verses I picked, the Lord filled me with overwhelming joy as He showed me this passage of scripture. I will hold onto it as I continue to pray.

Maybe you aren't necessarily praying for your future home, but it is never too late to start praying for the home in which you currently reside. The Lord will direct you as you pray.

Day 55

Amos 4:12-13

12 "Therefore this is what I will do to you, Israel, and because I will do this to you, Israel, prepare to meet your God." 13 He who forms the mountains, who creates the wind, and who reveals his thoughts to mankind, who turns dawn to darkness, and treads on the heights of the earth— the Lord God Almighty is his name.

Don't mess with God! :) I love the boldness with which the Lord proclaims who He is to those in this world. There is no insecurity or questioning of His motives. Aren't you glad that you serve a God who knows who you are on both the good and bad days? You don't have to question whether He is going to come through for you. He also is not afraid to show his wrath to those who come against Him. He lays it out for us.

We don't always know what is best for us. Prepare to meet your God if you so choose to do it your own way!

DAY 56

Amos 5:24
24 "But let justice roll on like a river, righteousness like a never-failing stream."

This is a gorgeous verse. It paints a picture of how the Lord
desires to pour out his righteousness and justice in this world.
Close your eyes and just imagine with me a never-failing stream of
righteousness. What do you see? What is the Lord revealing to you?

When I think of a never-failing stream of righteousness, I
think of Heaven. May His river of justice and never-failing stream
of righteousness be poured out on you today. May you touch a
piece of Heaven as you think upon His out-pouring!

DAY 57

Ezekiel 36:23

23 I will show the holiness of my great name, which has been profaned among the nations, the name you have profaned among them. Then the nations will know that I am the Lord, declares the Sovereign Lord, when I am proved holy through you before their eyes.

am so thankful that our God is not a God who shrinks back in fear when his name has been profaned. Instead, he is a God who rises up and shows himself holy. His name will be glorified even in negative circumstances. He can use weak people, ones who have made mistakes or even those who have actively walked in sin. He uses me. He uses you.

He says, "Then the nations will know that I am the LORD… when I am proven holy through you before their eyes." He proves his holiness right before their eyes. How will He use you today to make His holiness known among the nations?

Day 58

Nehemiah 4:19-20

19 Then I said to the nobles, the officials and the rest of the people, "The work is extensive and spread out, and we are widely separated from each other along the wall. 20 Wherever you hear the sound of the trumpet, join us there. Our God will fight for us!"

What a great leader Nehemiah is for the people. He wasn't afraid to proclaim the big picture. No, he didn't necessarily give the details of the project in these two verses, but he knew enough to know that the work was extensive and getting the job done would be difficult when the workers were spread out from one another. He gave clear direction. He gave them a signal to tell them when they were to come together. But he didn't just tell them to come together and begin the battle in their own strength as a team. He said, "The Lord will fight for you." Do you think you would be able to come together with others on a project and work together if you know the Lord is fighting for you?

For me, knowing that the Lord is fighting for me, totally changes my mindset regarding team work. It changes how I communicate and serve my team members. It gives me confidence to be aware of my fleshly tendencies that would keep me from wanting to do a certain task in completing the project. Team work should be about serving one another to get the job done, whether it is a secular or ministry job. If we go into it knowing the Lord is fighting for us, then we will be able to accomplish all the more!

DAY 59

Psalm 98:1

1 Sing to the Lord a new song, for he has done
marvelous things; his right hand and his holy
arm have worked salvation for him.

I am not a morning person, so this verse is a little too chipper for
my liking. I know, you are probably thinking, "This verse doesn't
say anything about the morning". But honestly, what if we were
to start our mornings off with singing the Lord a new song and
thinking upon the marvelous things He has done? Wouldn't that
turn our day around?

I leave you with this question to think upon: In what ways
has the Lord's right hand and holy arm worked out salvation in
your life?

DAY 60

Psalm 98:2-3

2 The Lord has made his salvation known and revealed his righteousness to the nations. 3 He has remembered his love and his faithfulness to Israel; all the ends of the earth have seen the salvation of our God.

This world is so troubled. It is easy to get focused on the negative and wonder if things will ever turn around. I think the Lord puts verses like these in the Bible so we can look to His Word and have hope for the world. The Lord is making His salvation known. He remembers his love and faithfulness. He doesn't forget. His salvation will be seen all the way to the ends of the earth. That's a promise!

DAY 61

Psalm 98:4-6

4 Shout for joy to the Lord, all the earth, burst into jubilant song with music; 5 make music to the Lord with the harp, with the harp and the sound of singing, 6 with trumpets and the blast of the ram's horn— shout for joy before the Lord, the King.

Now this would be one loud celebration! Praise the Lord that He even tells us how to celebrate Him! How awesome is that?! Just celebrate the Lord, the King, today!!! He is giving us permission to be loud!

DAY 62

Psalm 98:7-9

7 Let the sea resound, and everything in it, the world, and all who live in it. 8 Let the rivers clap their hands, let the mountains sing together for joy; 9 let them sing before the Lord, for he comes to judge the earth. He will judge the world in righteousness and the peoples with equity.

I don't think you can read these three verses without smiling. If you can, well I pray that the Lord will break through that which is stealing your joy.

Take a moment and reread the verses.

Did you read them?

Okay read them once more!

Do you realize that the Lord has taken 6 out of 9 verses of Psalm 98 just to tell His people and His creation how to celebrate and praise Him? All because He is making His salvation known throughout the earth!

Day 63

Acts 9:5

5 "Who are you, Lord?" Saul asked. "I am Jesus, whom you are persecuting," he replied.

Hmm…this verse is intriguing to me, but I am not fully sure how to wrap my brain around it. How many times a day do I persecute or speak against the Lord? This is a hard question to ask ourselves, but necessary so that we might walk in the light.

Day 64

Acts 9:9
9 For three days he was blind and did not eat or
drink anything.

Have you ever done a study on how many times the number three is referenced throughout scripture? The number three equals completion and in a quick google search, it is used 467 times in God's word. This is a random fact, but kind of a cool thought to consider.

When you think about the fact that Jesus rose from the dead after three days and Saul was blind for three days, you can see so many instances where the number three was so important to the Lord. He desires to bring completion to things. No, it may not always look like what we expect! That is where we get to step out and trust the Lord for His will!

Day 65

Acts 9:11-12

11 The Lord told him, "Go to the house of Judas on Straight Street and ask for a man from Tarsus named Saul, for he is praying. 12 In a vision he has seen a man named Ananias come and place his hands on him to restore his sight."

Ananias was the answer to Saul's prayers. The Lord was so clear in His directions to Ananias — even down to the street name. God cares about the details and as we pray, He directs.

Has the Lord given you a promise? Are you trusting Him to fulfill that promise? This is a reminder that His timing is perfect and we can trust Him to direct our path and bring together the necessary circumstances in the fulfillment of that promise… nothing is impossible for God!

My prayer: I don't know how you, Lord, are going to fulfill the promise you have given me, but I will pray and believe that I will see the fulfillment of this vision – in YOUR time and in YOUR way.

DAY 66

Acts 9:16

16 I will show him how much he must suffer
for my name."

What a beautifully rich verse to have a Heavenly Father who cares so deeply that He would hand pick us out of our sin and call us His instruments (v. 15) and then be so intimate with us that He would reveal how we will suffer for His name. I am loved! And so are you!

DAY 67

Acts 9:22

22 Yet Saul grew more and more powerful and baffled the Jews living in Damascus by proving that Jesus is the Messiah.

This is just really crazy to me to see the hand of God moving so powerfully through Saul! As Saul did the work of the Lord, the Lord revealed more and more of His power through him. How is the Lord showing His power through you? It is always good to reflect upon such thoughts to help keep our focus on the Lord and who He is in us

DAY 68

Acts 9:26

26 When he came to Jerusalem, he tried to join the disciples, but they were all afraid of him, not believing that he really was a disciple.

W hy were the disciples afraid of him? Hadn't they heard of God's hand upon Saul and how Saul was God's instrument? We may choose to fear our brothers and sisters around us. We are all human so we are guaranteed to make mistakes. Fear of man can close us off from so many opportunities and people that the Lord wants to use in our lives — regardless of our positive or negative first impressions.

Over the last few years, I have really learned to see the Lord's hand in my relationships with people. It helps me to not fear them, but rather to look at them as a son or daughter of the Most High God. Learning this is a process.

DAY 69

Acts 9:31

31 Then the church throughout Judea, Galilee and Samaria enjoyed a time of peace and was strengthened. Living in the fear of the Lord and encouraged by the Holy Spirit, it increased in numbers. "…Living in the fear of the Lord and encouraged by the Holy Spirit…"

What an awesome way to live! Am I, or are we, living in the fear of the Lord and encouraged by the Holy Spirit? How much do I open myself up to others to know if I am being a representation of this lifestyle?

The above questions may not be comfortable ones to ask ourselves. There is the freedom to skip the questions and not answer them. If we answer them, though, I am sure we will learn something new about ourselves. Be strengthened in Him — not in what you think is the best, most comfortable, answer.

DAY 70

Acts 9:33-34

33 There he found a man named Aeneas, who was paralyzed and had been bedridden for eight years. 34 "Aeneas," Peter said to him, "Jesus Christ heals you. Get up and roll up your mat." Immediately Aeneas got up.

He immediately got up! This is so challenging to my heart. I am unsure what my reaction would be – would I have the faith to believe for healing if a well-known leader came up to me and said, "Jesus Christ heals you…"

We are given the freedom to choose. We are given the freedom to choose to walk by faith.

Do I have the faith to believe God to bring healing in my situations? If God so chooses to open the door in any given situation, will I have the faith to believe God for complete healing in that moment?

I need to wait upon the Lord and ask Him to prepare my heart to receive His healing. Is there something in your life that the Lord wants to heal?

DAY 71

Acts 9:42

42 This became known all over Joppa, and many
people believed in the Lord.

I love that the acts of healing are clearly brought back to the Lord.
The people turn to the Lord because they see what He has done
through His followers. I pray that the Lord will show you His
healing hand and that you will look to Him.

Remember this healing doesn't always have to be a type of
physical healing. Perhaps the Lord wants to heal a mindset you
hold regarding someone or something in your past? The Lord longs
for us to focus on Him and believe Him in the healing process.

Day 72

Acts 10:16

16 This happened three times, and immediately the sheet was taken back to heaven.

Acts 10:19-20

19 While Peter was still thinking about the vision, the Spirit said to him, "Simon, three[a] men are looking for you. 20 So get up and go downstairs. Do not hesitate to go with them, for I have sent them."

Acts 10:30

30 Cornelius answered: "Three days ago I was in my house praying at this hour, at three in the afternoon. Suddenly a man in shining clothes stood before me

I find these different references to the number three very encouraging because it is a reminder of how God confirms and brings completion.

A few days ago we talked about the use of the number "three" in the Bible and these verses are more examples of that. He will complete His work in each of us. There is hope and He doesn't give up on us.

DAY 73

Acts 10:25-26

25 As Peter entered the house, Cornelius met him and fell at his feet in reverence. 26 But Peter made him get up. "Stand up," he said, "I am only a man myself."

I just love Peter's response. Peter is so to the point, yet there is a sense of humility as well. Know who you are and live with a mindset of humility toward those around you.

This principle applies even when you go into a meeting or when you are working with others. We can get so caught up in the position we have been given. It is good to know your position. But a good leader or teammate is one who acts with humility.

DAY 74

Acts 10:28

28 He said to them: "You are well aware that it is against our law for a Jew to associate with or visit a Gentile. But God has shown me that I should not call anyone impure or unclean.

This is one way to remove judgmental thoughts toward others. It is so easy to think of others as being impure and unclean. As humans in this fallen world, we use that mindset as our filter in looking at others. None of us are perfect. But, how beautiful would it be if we were to think or look at people around us as clean and pure?

May the Lord give us the grace to reset our filter.

DAY 75

Acts 10:34-35

34 Then Peter began to speak: "I now realize how true it is that God does not show favoritism 35 but accepts from every nation the one who fears him and does what is right.

D oes it really say this in the Bible?!?! How great are these two verses?! Any verse to do with fearing the Lord is always good. I am so thankful that the Lord doesn't show favoritism. All He asks is that we fear Him and do what is right. When I think of other people in light of these verses, it really changes my perspective — and I view others as equal to me. They are no better than I am and I am no better than they are. But, in this judgmental and individualistic society, it is easy to think that we are the favored one in the sight of God.

This verse changes that thought.

Lord, help me and help each of us to look at one another through your eyes. You don't favor one over the other. May we trust you to help us work out our differences or misunderstandings. Oh, that we would fear you and do what is right. Amen.

Day 76

Micah 6:8

8 He has shown you, O mortal, what is good. And what does the Lord require of you? To act justly and to love mercy and to walk humbly[a] with your God.

What does it mean to really live out Micah 6:8? To act justly and to love mercy and to walk humbly with your God?

If I think about it, it is all a domino effect. We can't act justly without loving mercy. We can't walk with humility and not love mercy. But, these questions above are ones that we can only answer for ourselves and not for someone else. We must be willing to take these questions before the Lord and seek Him, asking Him to reveal to us the condition of our heart.

May you have an open heart and open ears to hear what the Lord would have for you today as you ask Him for answers to these questions. His answer will come in His perfect time—that may not be today, but it will come. Trust Him!

Day 77

Micah 6:3-4

3 "My people, what have I done to you? How have I burdened you? Answer me. 4 I brought you up out of Egypt and redeemed you from the land of slavery. I sent Moses to lead you, also Aaron and Miriam.

God asks a beautiful question, "How have I burdened you?" I love the blunt questions of God. I imagine He may have asked this question with some sadness in His voice. What was the tone of His voice?

Life is tough. It doesn't always go the way we want it to go. Today, you may be having a great day or maybe it is a rough day. Nothing seems to be going as planned. Whatever feelings you are experiencing today, I encourage you to think upon this question that the Lord asks, "How have I burdened you?" I pray that the Spirit of God will lead you into a deep and merciful place!

DAY 78

Micah 6:5

5 My people, remember what Balak king of
Moab plotted and what Balaam son of Beor
answered. Remember your journey from Shittim
to Gilgal, that you may know the righteous acts
of the Lord."

"Remember your journey…that you may know the righteous
acts of the Lord." Remember where God has brought you
from. Remember. Remember. Remember. Don't forget the Lord.
Take a moment today and just remember!

DAY 79

Jeremiah 28:7-9

7 Nevertheless, listen to what I have to say in your hearing and in the hearing of all the people: 8 From early times the prophets who preceded you and me have prophesied war, disaster and plague against many countries and great kingdoms. 9 But the prophet who prophesies peace will be recognized as one truly sent by the LORD only if his prediction comes true."

Jeremiah 29:4-14

4 This is what the LORD Almighty, the God of Israel, says to all those I carried into exile from Jerusalem to Babylon: 5 "Build houses and settle down; plant gardens and eat what they produce. 6 Marry and have sons and daughters; find wives for your sons and give your daughters in marriage, so that they too may have sons and daughters. Increase in number there; do not decrease. 7 Also, seek the peace and prosperity of the city to which I have carried you into exile. Pray to the LORD for it, because if it prospers, you too will prosper." 8 Yes, this is what the LORD Almighty, the God of Israel, says: "Do not let the prophets and diviners among you deceive you. Do not

listen to the dreams you encourage them to have. 9 They are prophesying lies to you in my name. I have not sent them," declares the LORD.

10 This is what the LORD says: "When seventy years are completed for Babylon, I will come to you and fulfill my good promise to bring you back to this place. 11 For I know the plans I have for you," declares the LORD, "plans to prosper you and not to harm you, plans to give you hope and a future. 12 Then you will call on me and come and pray to me, and I will listen to you. 13 You will seek me and find me when you seek me with all your heart. 14 I will be found by you," declares the LORD, "and will bring you back from captivity. I will gather you from all the nations and places where I have banished you," declares the LORD, "and will bring you back to the place from which I carried you into exile."

It is really cool to read Jeremiah 29 in context with chapter 28. God is carrying the people into exile after all that has been falsely prophesied to them in previous chapters. But even in their exile, God promises that He has a plan to give them a hope and a future. Those who seek Him will find Him and He will carry them out of the exile.

DAY 80

Acts 12:19

19 After Herod had a thorough search made for him and did not find him, he cross-examined the guards and ordered that they be executed.

Wow! This is terrible. Was this order of Herod's carried out? Were the guards executed?

I know this isn't the most uplifting verse to be reading in a devotional, but it makes us aware of those who are in power around us. It is easy to drown out the chaos of the world and our disappointment in how different leaders are leading nations. But if we just sit back and do nothing, then we aren't really helping.

We have the opportunity to pray to the Almighty God and ask Him to do big and mighty things to change this world. I would encourage you to ask the Lord for the faith to pray for those things which you have seen on the news recently or to pray for things going on in your kids' schools. He is waiting with open arms for us to come and talk with Him!

Day 81

Acts 11:17-18

17 So if God gave them the same gift he gave us who believed in the Lord Jesus Christ, who was I to think that I could stand in God's way?" 18 When they heard this, they had no further objections and praised God, saying, "So then, even to Gentiles God has granted repentance that leads to life.

These verses are so encouraging to me when I think about various people in my life. God has given me the gift of the Holy Spirit and repentance. He has given my fellow brother and sister believers that same gift. So who am I to think that I could get in God's way? God has the power to change my heart and mind. He can do the same for you. God wants us both to have life.

My prayer is that I would not get in God's way. I think each of us could probably insert an individual's name here, someone we would not want to see get in the way of God's work either. Don't be afraid to make this personal today and pray that the Lord will keep you from getting in His way of changing who He wants you to be in Him.

DAY 82

Acts 11:8-9

8 "I replied, 'Surely not, Lord! Nothing impure or unclean has ever entered my mouth.'

9 "The voice spoke from heaven a second time, 'Do not call anything impure that God has made clean.'

I was reading through chapter 11 and totally missed these two verses until after reading verses 17-18. I so often get stuck on what a person did to me and how he or she wronged me. It's those wrong actions that I see and play over in my mind, that make me question whether or not a person has changed. I even feel anxious when I consider meeting with this person with the purpose of attempting to restore the relationship. But, verses 8 and 9 are great reminders that God has made my brother or sister clean no matter what sin they have committed just as I have been made clean no matter what sin I have committed. I need to not focus on what is "unclean or impure" and focus more on who people are in Christ and what God calls clean.

DAY 83

Acts 3:19

19 Repent, then, and turn to God, so that your
sins may be wiped out, that times of refreshing
may come from the Lord,

I n light of Acts 11:8-9, the Lord reminded me of this verse that
He had shown me a number of years ago while I was walking
through a situation with an individual. The Lord used this verse
to show me that if we each repent, our sins will be wiped out and
there will be refreshing!

This verse becomes foundational when working through any
situation with another person you feel has wronged you. God
desires to love us deeply and wipe our sins away — to make us
clean. This act of repentance is to be between the Lord and me.
The other person's act of repentance is to be between him and the
Lord. It is not either your or my judgment, but we can certainly ask
the Lord for His will to be done and ask Him to give us a spirit of
forgiveness toward the other person.

DAY 84

Acts 11:23

23 When he arrived and saw what the grace of
God had done, he was glad and encouraged them
all to remain true to the Lord with all their hearts.

It is all about what the grace of God did — not what man did —
nor what a group of people did; it is about what the LORD did. I
love that this is the encouragement that was brought to the body of
Christ. It's so simple! Remain true to the Lord with all your hearts.

Do I do that? Do I remain true to the Lord? How do I remain
true to the Lord with all my heart? What does this look like? In
reading this verse, I sense that God wants to help me grow, specifically in this area. What about you?

DAY 85

Acts 11:26

26 and when he found him, he brought him to
Antioch. So for a whole year Barnabas and Saul
met with the church and taught great numbers
of people. The disciples were called Christians
first at Antioch.

What a commitment! This is so very exciting and
refreshing! They spent a whole year in this region, just
teaching the body of Christ about the Lord. They dedicated a year
to learning more about Jesus. In your sphere of influence, who can
you disciple? Or maybe you are the one in need of being discipled?
Are we willing to make ourselves available to others to speak the
love of God into their lives? Are we willing to open ourselves to
His searching of our hearts? How can we break out of that " don't
want to bother anyone because they are too busy" mindset and just
be a blessing to others? God created fellowship among believers
for a reason!

Day 86

Acts 12:2
2 He had James, the brother of John, put to death
with the sword.

I don't know that I knew this is how James died.
Today's devotional is more of an interesting Bible fact. I would encourage you to read chapter 12 as the next few days will be more directed toward this chapter. May this be a day to simply ask the Lord to prepare you for whatever He wants to teach you through this chapter.

DAY 87

Acts 12:5

5 So Peter was kept in prison, but the church was earnestly praying to God for him.

HA! What in the world?!?! This is so encouraging! How crazy would it have been to be a part of those prayer times with the body of Christ? Wow!

There are many throughout the world who have been persecuted for their faith and are now in prison. We may not know them by name, but the Lord does. Take some time today to pray for those who are in prison. Ask the Lord to show you if there is anything specific that you can be praying for on behalf of our brothers and sisters. As you pray, keep verse 5 in mind — it just may be what you need to persevere in praying for those who are imprisoned.

DAY 88

Acts 12:9

9 Peter followed him out of the prison, but he had no idea that what the angel was doing was really happening; he thought he was seeing a vision.

I can't imagine being hit in the side to be woken up and then just walking out of prison with some guy. I would probably have thought it was some kind of vision too. I mean that is a pretty sweet vision to be having anyways, but then to actually be living it out?!?! That is so awesome!

No, I have never been in prison, but I have had so many moments with the Lord where He has done something and I think, "Is this for real?" It is the Lord moving on my behalf. What has the Lord done on your behalf?

DAY 89

Acts 12:11

11 Then Peter came to himself and said, "Now I know without a doubt that the Lord has sent his angel and rescued me from Herod's clutches and from everything the Jewish people were hoping would happen."

I hope someday I will be able to have an "aha" moment like this. That's not to say that I haven't already had many of those throughout the years — but AHA — can you imagine?!?! The day the Lord completely brings about the fulfillment of a promise He has given — it will be totally worth all the hard work and prayer it took to get to that place of victory!

Keep trusting the Lord.

DAY 90

Acts 12:15

15 "You're out of your mind," they told her.
When she kept insisting that it was so, they said,
"It must be his angel."

I f you look back to verse 12, the Bible refers to these people as
people who had "gathered and were praying". So, how many
times do we, as believers, pray on our own or gather to pray with
others and yet — we doubt? Doesn't God's word say where two
or three are gathered, there He is in our midst? What's the deal?
These people had gathered to pray AND earlier in this chapter it
talks about how Peter was sent to prison and the CHURCH was
EARNESTLY praying to God for him!!!! Earnestly praying!!!!
And yet, they doubt. I pray. But do I pray with expectancy, waiting
for God to move?

Do I pray for hearts to be changed with the expectancy that
God will or IS CURRENTLY moving in a person's heart? Do I
pray with expectancy that God is really going to do what he says
He will do when he impresses a promise upon my heart and asks
me to trust him? Do I pray with expectancy that God is going to
direct my future paths?

The Lord has given you and me different promises, so we can
trust that he will give us all the pieces to see that particular promise
fulfilled. We should be praying with expectancy. Lord, help our
unbelief — right?

Day 91

Acts 12:23-24

23 Immediately, because Herod did not give praise to God, an angel of the Lord struck him down, and he was eaten by worms and died. 24 But the word of God continued to spread and flourish.

Ummm dude, this is just gross!!!! Who dies this way?!?! Like seriously!!!! Note to self: Praise the Lord…otherwise you will be struck down and eaten by worms…and die.

OH but WAIT!!!!!! Then there is verse 24!!! HA–it's so great!!!!! But the word of God continued to spread! So, God may kill off men in power who are evil, but HIS WORD is still going to go forth and flourish!!!!! What a breath of fresh air. When all seems evil and downcast — we can still turn to His word for hope!!!!!!!!!

DAY 92

Matthew 12:11-12

11 He said to them, "If any of you has a sheep and it falls into a pit on the Sabbath, will you not take hold of it and lift it out? 12 How much more valuable is a person than a sheep! Therefore it is lawful to do good on the Sabbath."

don't know why this passage sticks out to me, I can't really get my brain wrapped around it. It's just there and I feel like I need a deeper understanding of this passage.

Day 93

John 6:33

33 For the bread of God is the bread that comes down from heaven and gives life to the world."

This just paints a beautiful picture of who Jesus is and why God sent him to this earth. And yet, it shows His continuous dependence on His Father.

DAY 94

Ruth 2:3

3 So she went out, entered a field and began to glean behind the harvesters. As it turned out, she was working in a field belonging to Boaz, who was from the clan of Elimelek.

"Nothing happens by accident in God's economy. God is always orchestrating the plans of His people for their good and His glory."–David Platt

Ruth found herself in Boaz's field to pick barley.

Day 95

Isaiah 7:10-14

10 Again the Lord spoke to Ahaz, 11 "Ask the Lord your God for a sign, whether in the deepest depths or in the highest heights."

12 But Ahaz said, "I will not ask; I will not put the Lord to the test."

13 Then Isaiah said, "Hear now, you house of David! Is it not enough to try the patience of humans? Will you try the patience of my God also? 14 Therefore the Lord himself will give you[a] a sign: The virgin[b] will conceive and give birth to a son, and[c] will call him Immanuel.[d]

It just totally blows me away that God flat out asks Ahaz, "Ask the Lord your God to give you a sign…", which Ahaz refuses. But then the sign ends up being the prophecy of Jesus's coming.

ASK THE LORD FOR SIGNS!

DAY 96

Obadiah 1:12-15

12 You should not gloat over your brother in the day of his misfortune, nor rejoice over the people of Judah in the day of their destruction, nor boast so much in the day of their trouble. 13 You should not march through the gates of my people in the day of their disaster, nor gloat over them in their calamity in the day of their disaster, nor seize their wealth in the day of their disaster. 14 You should not wait at the crossroads to cut down their fugitives, nor hand over their survivors in the day of their trouble

15 "The day of the Lord is near for all nations. As you have done, it will be done to you; your deeds will return upon your own head.

Don't gloat in the day of their disaster! What you have done will be done to you!

Day 97

Genesis 9:12-17

12 And God said, "This is the sign of the covenant I am making between me and you and every living creature with you, a covenant for all generations to come: 13 I have set my rainbow in the clouds, and it will be the sign of the covenant between me and the earth.14 Whenever I bring clouds over the earth and the rainbow appears in the clouds, 15 I will remember my covenant between me and you and all living creatures of every kind. Never again will the waters become a flood to destroy all life. 16 Whenever the rainbow appears in the clouds, I will see it and remember the everlasting covenant between God and all living creatures of every kind on the earth." 17 So God said to Noah, "This is the sign of the covenant I have established between me and all life on the earth."

God says, "I have set my rainbow", as a reminder for himself and all living creatures on this earth. May we be reminded of God's faithfulness and covenant as we look to the clouds and see the rainbow after a storm.

This is a beautiful reminder for when we go through the storms of life as well. Sometimes we go through really tough days. The storm is filled with pouring-down rain and flashes of lightning. During a storm, we may not be able to see how to move forward. But there is hope! We can look to Genesis 9:12-17 and ask the Lord to help us see the rainbow! He will be faithful to show us as we trust Him!

Day 98

Nehemiah 7:5
5 So my God put it into my heart to assemble the nobles, the officials and the common people for registration by families…

How beautiful that Nehemiah acknowledges the presence of God. It is God who put the idea in his heart to register the families. Are we acknowledging that the Lord is the one who has placed different plans in our heart and are we walking in obedience to those plans, seeking Him for His perfect timing?

DAY 99

Esther 4:12-16

12 When Esther's words were reported to Mordecai, 13 he sent back this answer: "Do not think that because you are in the king's house you alone of all the Jews will escape. 14 For if you remain silent at this time, relief and deliverance for the Jews will arise from another place, but you and your father's family will perish. And who knows but that you have come to your royal position for such a time as this?"

15 Then Esther sent this reply to Mordecai: 16 "Go, gather together all the Jews who are in Susa, and fast for me. Do not eat or drink for three days, night or day. I and my attendants will fast as you do. When this is done, I will go to the king, even though it is against the law. And if I perish, I perish."

I have heard "For such a time as this...", preached many times by one of my leaders. But reading it today, just brings so much peace to my heart because it is a great and clear proof that we don't know God's timing or place. But He has our future in His hands.

God has called us to be obedient. I could be prideful about how obedient I have been in this season, but it is so not about me because I daily fall short of God's glory. This passage is yet another "scripture" barrier which God is breaking down and showing me how it practically applies to my life.

"And who knows but that you have come to your royal position for such a time as this." I love how Mordecai acknowledges our lack of knowing God's plans and timing. There are so many things in this season of which I can't explain the "why", but only to exclaim... "But God!" Then continue on to verse 16, where Esther replies and wants all the Jews to go before the Lord in fasting and prayer on her behalf because she knew it would go against the law and society to go before the King when she wasn't invited.

She acknowledges the power of God, "fast for me. Do not eat or drink for three days, night or day. I and my attendants will do the same as you do. When this is done, I will go to the king, even though it is against the law. And if I perish, I perish." (v. 16) If she dies then she dies for the glory of the Lord, not for any human glory. Obedience to the Lord does amount to "death to self", maybe not physical death, but she did have to say "no" to the human law and follow God.

DAY 100

Psalm 127:4
4 Like arrows in the hands of a warrior are children born in one's youth.

I am not sure how to comprehend Psalm 127:4. Is this meant to be
a good or bad portrayal? This is a verse to just ponder for today.
See how the Lord speaks to you regarding the children in your life.

Day 101

Ecclesiastes 1:18
18 For with much wisdom comes much sorrow;
the more knowledge, the more grief.

This verse is so true. In our culture today we think and are told that if we knew this information or read this new book, then we would know it all. But I like what Francis Chan said in his book, You and Me Forever, about how the world says we need this new book or whatever and we have all this knowledge, yet we don't put much of it into practice.

In many ways, the more knowledge we have about something, can truly bring more grief and become meaningless.

DAY 102

Numbers 16:20-22

20 The Lord said to Moses and Aaron, 21 "Separate yourselves from this assembly so I can put an end to them at once."

22 But Moses and Aaron fell face down and cried out, "O God, the God who gives breath to all living things, will you be angry with the entire assembly when only one man sins?"

Woah! How crazy is it that Moses and Aaron fall face down and plead for the assembly?! God is the God who gives breath to all living things. Will He be angry with everyone because of one man's sin?

DAY 103

Acts 13:2-3

2 While they were worshiping the Lord and fasting, the Holy Spirit said, "Set apart for me Barnabas and Saul for the work to which I have called them." 3 So after they had fasted and prayed, they placed their hands on them and sent them off.

When I first read these verses, my thought was, "Such obedience". :) And then as I looked at the verses closer, the picture of their obedience to the Holy Spirit became even more clear! Not only were they obedient to what the Holy Spirit called them to do, but then in verse 3, it doesn't say "they watched TV and did this or that and then sent them off." No—they finished praying and fasting and THEN sent them off.

This is kind of what my Pastor was talking about in one of his recent messages, "Often there are so many good things put before us to do (and yes they are probably put there by the Holy Spirit) but then we get distracted from the BEST things that God has for us. They didn't just stop what they were doing and send them off. No, they finished what they were doing." (Paraphrase mine) They finished the BEST thing first and then sent them off.

Would the results of Barnabas and Saul's ministry have been the same if the people heard the word from the Holy Spirit and just jumped on what was said? Or was their ministry that much more fruitful because they finished praying and fasting before they moved in obedience?

Has the Lord given you a word on which you should obediently act? If I were to just take the good word or promise God gives me and step out without asking God to walk me through the steps of preparation — praying, fasting, spending time in His Word, learning from others — then I would miss out on what God wants to teach me.

It is so much better to sit and wait upon the Lord and oh, be faithful where you are. The Lord will bring deliverance! Yeah–that totally just happened! Praise God!

DAY 104

Acts 13:7

7 who was an attendant of the proconsul, Sergius
Paulus. The proconsul, an intelligent man, sent
for Barnabas and Saul because he wanted to hear
the word of God.

This verse is just super cool! This guy is an attendant of the evil
one and yet, he wants to hear the word of God!!! Talk about
the Lord hand picking us!!!!

DAY 105

Acts 13:9-10

9 Then Saul, who was also called Paul, filled with the Holy Spirit, looked straight at Elymas and said, 10 "You are a child of the devil and an enemy of everything that is right! You are full of all kinds of deceit and trickery. Will you never stop perverting the right ways of the Lord?

The power of the Holy Spirit is crazy!!! I LOVE that it says that Paul looked straight at this child of the devil and called him out on his perversion of the right ways of the Lord. The enemy is going to have a hey-day with each one of us and try to make us doubt the ways of the Lord. But, how great is it that we can hold onto the promises of our Heavenly Daddy, our Abba Father, the Beginning and the End?

So I look at these verses in Acts and it is just a reminder that I can look at the devil straight in the face and BOLDLY proclaim that he is perverting the right ways of the Lord and he has no place in my mind because God's got this. He has overcome and already given me the victory!!!

Day 106

Acts 13:12

12 When the proconsul saw what had happened, he believed, for he was amazed at the teaching about the Lord.

Praise the Lord!!! God planted the seed and now this guy is following Him!!! I would encourage you to take some time to praise the Lord for the different seeds He has planted in your life or in the lives of those around you! The Lord is good and calls us to rejoice in His ways!

DAY 107

Acts 13:22

22 After removing Saul, he made David their king. God testified concerning him: 'I have found David son of Jesse, a man after my own heart; he will do everything I want him to do.'

If I were to personalize this verse and put my name in it, "...God testified concerning her: 'I have found Shareen daughter of Neil, a woman after my own heart; she will do everything I want her to do.'" WHAT!?!? That holds some major weight and a pair of massive shoes to fill for sure.

I also find it interesting that the "son of Jesse" is put in there. That was probably some kind of cultural thing at that time, but then when I personalize it, it has a whole different take. Would God testify that I, a daughter of Neil, am a woman after His own heart? A woman who will do whatever He wants me to do?

I am stuck on this "son of" thing. So, David is someone who watched over his father's flock. He was trusted with his father's flock and then on top of that, didn't Jesse present David to Saul?

I know I can hold onto the promise that God knows me and I am known by God. But, is that enough for me? It should be.

DAY 108

Acts 13:34

34 God raised him from the dead so that he will never be subject to decay. As God has said, "'I will give you the holy and sure blessings promised to David.'

W hy would you not want to be a believer when you have a promise like this to hold on to? The holiness and purity that springs forth from this verse is so refreshing. Praise the Lord!

DAY 109

Acts 13:36
36 "Now when David had served God's purpose in his own generation, he fell asleep; he was buried with his ancestors and his body decayed.

When I read this verse, it just made me think of my Granddad. When my Granddad served God's purpose in his own generation, he fell asleep. How sweet of a promise is this? Yes, the end of this verse talks about how our bodies are going to decay, but it's a sweet thing to know that when we have served God's purpose — not my purpose, not my boss's purpose, not my parents' purpose — no, God's purpose, we will fall asleep. We get to spend eternity with our Heavenly Daddy. That is a day worth living for. The day that I get to crawl up in my Heavenly Daddy's lap because He has called me home for eternity.

DAY 110

Acts 13:41

41 "'Look, you scoffers, wonder and perish, for I am going to do something in your days that you would never believe, even if someone told you.'"

When you read this verse, what does it say to you? The power of God is so evident. He is not one who will shrink back, but rather boldly proclaim that He will do things that the scoffers will not believe even if someone were to tell them about it. This verse just pops out to me for some reason. It gives me something to ponder and I hope it does for you as well.

DAY 111

Acts 13:43

43 When the congregation was dismissed, many
of the Jews and devout converts to Judaism followed Paul and Barnabas, who talked with them
and urged them to continue in the grace of God.

What does it look like to "continue in the grace of God"?
That would be a good thing to actively be praying for.
"Lord, please help me to continue in your grace."

I don't know about you, but I am not very good at accepting
grace from others the Lord has placed in my life or giving myself
grace, especially when I am facing difficult or trying situations.
This verse is a great reminder to actively ask the Lord to help me
grow in that grace that He lavishes on me day and night.

Day 112

Acts 13:46-48

46 Then Paul and Barnabas answered them boldly: "We had to speak the word of God to you first. Since you reject it and do not consider yourselves worthy of eternal life, we now turn to the Gentiles. 47 For this is what the Lord has commanded us: "'I have made you[f] a light for the Gentiles, that you may bring salvation to the ends of the earth.'" 48 When the Gentiles heard this, they were glad and honored the word of the Lord; and all who were appointed for eternal life believed.

I can't imagine having a mindset that I am not worthy of eternal life, but maybe that is, in some ways, what I am saying when I doubt who I am in Christ or that I am worth the investment. I mean, God calls us His children which means we are worthy of eternal life.

That is such a great command from the Lord. "I have made you a light for the Gentiles that you may bring salvation to the ends of the earth." This is what the Church is supposed to be. God commands us and says He MADE us to be a light. We don't have to figure out HOW to be a light. He made us this way to preach the word of God to the ends of the earth. That's a challenge for sure.

The question for me is, am I willing to be the light for him that God made me to be? All who were appointed for eternal life believed. Praise God! That is truly the hand of God.

DAY 113

Acts 13:52
52 And the disciples were filled with joy and
with the Holy Spirit.

I love that this chapter 13 starts and ends with the Holy Spirit.
When we see the work of the Lord, we should be filled with
joy and the Holy Spirit. This verse challenges me to look at each
day and embrace the joy that I have in the Lord and to embrace
the Holy Spirit. And it is the Lord who gives me the time to be
in the Word. It is also the Lord who has spoken to me as I have
gone through His Word. The Lord is the one moving each of
us forward!

DAY 114

Acts 14:2-3

2 But the Jews who refused to believe stirred up the other Gentiles and poisoned their minds against the brothers. 3 So Paul and Barnabas spent considerable time there, speaking boldly for the Lord, who confirmed the message of his grace by enabling them to perform signs and wonders.

The Jews poisoned the Gentiles' minds. This sounds like what I have experienced in ministry with those who are against the work of the Lord. They have refused to believe and seek out truth. From there, they have poisoned others' minds.

But, then there is verse 3! I love that even though the devil is out to kill, steal, and destroy, the Lord is still on HIS throne and brings victory! I love that Paul and Barnabas's reaction to the stirring up of trouble was to spend time speaking boldly for the Lord. The end of verse 3 talks about the outpouring of God's grace. Even though evil was intended, the confirmation of the message of God's grace still went forward!

DAY 115

Acts 14:9

9 He listened to Paul as he was speaking. Paul looked directly at him, saw that he had faith to be healed.

What does faith look like? How could Paul tell just by looking at this man that he had faith to be healed? Do I look at others around me as though they have faith to believe? Or do I look at them as though they doubt?

These are questions I need to continuously ask myself. I hope that they are an encouragement to you as you press into the Lord today. We can ask these questions of ourselves in our own strength, but the best answer will come as we seek the Lord and trust Him to show us His perspective on these questions.

Day 116

Acts 14:15-17

15 "Friends, why are you doing this? We too are only human, like you. We are bringing you good news, telling you to turn from these worthless things to the living God, who made the heavens and the earth and the sea and everything in them. 16 In the past, he let all nations go their own way. 17 Yet he has not left himself without testimony: He has shown kindness by giving you rain from heaven and crops in their seasons; he provides you with plenty of food and fills your hearts with joy."

They call their enemies "friends". This is a reminder of what I would like to say to anyone who is bringing disunity to the body of Christ or anyone who would persecute the work of the Lord. It is hard for me to understand why someone would want to live their life tearing down that of the Lord's ordination.

The Lord has only given us good things and filled our hearts with joy.

DAY 117

Acts 14:19-20

19 Then some Jews came from Antioch and Iconium and won the crowd over. They stoned Paul and dragged him outside the city, thinking he was dead. 20 But after the disciples had gathered around him, he got up and went back into the city. The next day he and Barnabas left for Derbe.

Nothing can stop these guys! The Lord just continues to use them. How awesome is that?! Whatever the enemy tries to put in front of you today, just remember this testimony of Paul's life and keep pressing forward.

The Lord has already given you the victory!

DAY 118

Acts 14:22

22 strengthening the disciples and encouraging
them to remain true to the faith. "We must go
through many hardships to enter the kingdom
of God," they said.

This is a refreshing piece of advice! If I could remember this
verse when I am facing a trial, that would be very helpful. The
trials we face are worth it, knowing we will someday be in the
kingdom of heaven for eternity!

My prayer for us today: "Lord, please help each of us to
remember that we must go through many hardships to enter the
kingdom of God. This is truly a beautiful promise that you have
given us to hold on to in this life."

DAY 119

Jeremiah 29:24-32

24 Tell Shemaiah the Nehelamite, 25 "This is what the Lord Almighty, the God of Israel, says: You sent letters in your own name to all the people in Jerusalem, to the priest Zephaniah son of Maaseiah, and to all the other priests. You said to Zephaniah, 26 'The Lord has appointed you priest in place of Jehoiada to be in charge of the house of the Lord; you should put any maniac who acts like a prophet into the stocks and neck-irons. 27 So why have you not reprimanded Jeremiah from Anathoth, who poses as a prophet among you? 28 He has sent this message to us in Babylon: It will be a long time. Therefore build houses and settle down; plant gardens and eat what they produce.'"

29 Zephaniah the priest, however, read the letter to Jeremiah the prophet. 30 Then the word of the Lord came to Jeremiah: 31 "Send this message to all the exiles: 'This is what the Lord says about Shemaiah the Nehelamite: Because Shemaiah has prophesied to you, even though I did not send him, and has persuaded you to trust in lies, 32 this is what the Lord says: I will

surely punish Shemaiah the Nehelamite and his
descendants. He will have no one left among this
people, nor will he see the good things I will do
for my people, declares the Lord, because he has
preached rebellion against me.'"

read this passage of scripture and it really struck me. I am still
seeking the Lord on how He wants to use these verses in my life,
but I felt I needed to add it to this devotional. I don't know how
the Lord wants to use this in your life today or in the future. I pray
that you will wait on the Lord and see what He will do.

Day 120

Romans 3:18

18 "There is no fear of God before their eyes."

This verse. It is so simple and yet so deep with the clear voice of God. As I read this verse I begin to think about my perception of life. I don't want to be a person who does not have the fear of God before my eyes.

I have a long way to go in order to grow in fearing the Lord, but I want to fear Him whether things go my way or not. I want to be a person who steps out in obedience to reconcile a wrong and if that reconciliation doesn't come from the other person — I want to have the fear of the Lord before my eyes. That is the only way to get through life. If you and I are able to fall back on that fear of the Lord, then we will be able to trust Him to carry us through even the deepest and darkest of hurts.

To be honest, when I first read this verse, I pointed fingers at those who have been against me or won't reconcile with me. I jumped on the train of judgment and said to myself, "is that person really looking through a perspective of fearing the Lord rather than man?" But then the Lord, in His grace, gently reminded me that I need to look at my own life and perspective. But even more importantly, the Lord showed me that I can use this verse as a tool to pray for those around me that they would have the fear of the Lord before their eyes as they go through life. And then entrust them to the Lord that He will move in and through them.

It is not in our own strength that we fear the Lord. It is by Him as we trust Him that we grow in having that fear of the Lord before our eyes.

Day 121

Romans 4:18-19

18 Against all hope, Abraham in hope believed and so became the father of many nations, just as it had been said to him, "So shall your offspring be."[d] 19 Without weakening in his faith, he faced the fact that his body was as good as dead—since he was about a hundred years old—and that Sarah's womb was also dead.

I love these verses because it is a great reminder that we can look at our circumstances that seem so hopeless, and yet trust the Lord beyond what they may seem. We don't have to go through life dependent on what we, in our limited human knowledge, know or don't know.

Verse 18 says, "Against all hope, Abraham in hope believed". He believed what God said to him no matter what he knew to be factual. I can look at circumstances in my life and tell myself over and over again, "This isn't going to happen. I don't see how this will ever come about. I hear God's promise, but how is this even going to be possible?" But having that mindset weakens my faith.

And honestly, I have seen the Lord come through
time and time again as I "in hope believed".

So, Lord, today — would you please help each one of us to
"in hope believe" You for the promises You have set before us? We
need your help. I need your help. Please help me not to weaken
my faith by looking at circumstances rather than what I know You
have told me. Amen

DAY 122

Romans 4:20-21

20 Yet he did not waver through unbelief regarding the promise of God, but was strengthened in his faith and gave glory to God, 21 being fully persuaded that God had power to do what he had promised.

W hat a way to live your life! To build on yesterday's devotional, these two verses have so much power in them. If all you do today is read verses 20-21 over and over again — I am positive that your mindset will change no matter what you have before you today!

Yes, you can choose to read these verses and say, "Woe is me. I am always wavering in unbelief." Or, you can read these verses and trust that your Heavenly Daddy has the "power to do what he has promised." (Verse 21)

It's a choice. What will you do for today? For the next 5 minutes? For the next hour? Will you choose to live in God's power or in your own thoughts? Trust me! This is a wake up call for me as well!

DAY 123

Romans 8:18

18 I consider that our present sufferings are not worth comparing with the glory that will be revealed in us.

The Lord used this verse in a very powerful way during my time away from ministry. I believe this verse truly speaks for itself. I don't say that to make light of anything you may be walking through, but there is nothing that compares with the glory to be revealed in us. The Lord is working in the mess and He is making each of us more like Him!

DAY 124

Romans 10:8-9

8 But what does it say? "The word is near you;
it is in your mouth and in your heart,"[a] that is,
the message concerning faith that we proclaim:
9 If you declare with your mouth, "Jesus is Lord,"
and believe in your heart that God raised him
from the dead, you will be saved.

How delightful are the promises of God's Word? Praise the Lord that His Word is near us. It is so near to us that it is in our mouth and our heart! I pray that today you will just allow Romans 10:8-9 to wash over every minuscule part of your day. I pray that we would face today as though we have the message of our faith to proclaim. May these verses make us walk upright and tall, with confidence, declaring that "Jesus is Lord"! May we live out today with faith in our hearts that our Heavenly Father has risen Christ from the dead!!!

Now go forth and conquer the world! Be in the world, but not of the world!

DAY 125

Romans 10:10
10 For it is with your heart that you believe and
are justified, and it is with your mouth that you
profess your faith and are saved.

Here's the thing, if you have any background in church, you
will know Romans 10:9. You may even have it memorized!
We can be so focused on verse 9 and totally miss out on the precious, deeply enriched, jewel that comes in verse 10.

"For it is with your heart that you believe and are justified, and
it is with your mouth that you profess your faith and are saved."
Yes! It is that good that I couldn't help myself but write it out again!
Take a moment and let the words of this verse just sink in.

Are the words deeply sunk into your mind? So listen to this:
As these words have sunk in, do you realize that this verse is proclaiming that our justification and our faith and salvation has
NOTHING to do with our minds? We don't believe with our
minds nor are we justified or even gain salvation by professing
what we hear on TV. No—we believe with our hearts and profess
with our mouths!!!

I just PRAISE GOD that our justification is based on what
we believe in our hearts and that God has created us to profess
with our mouths our faith that we are saved!

DAY 126

1 Corinthians 1:5
5 For in him you have been enriched in every way—with all kinds of speech and with all knowledge —

Whether you do your devotions in the morning or at night, this is a great promise to hold tightly to each and every day. Our Heavenly Daddy enriches us!

Doesn't that excite you? I hope it does!

This verse tells us that he does this for us in every way — He enriches our mouths and our minds. Because we are in Him, our thought life and our words are enriched. I don't know about you, but thinking about this makes me feel so empowered. The beautiful thing about it is that I don't feel empowered because of anything I have the capability to do — but because of Him. We could look at this verse and feel pretty good about ourselves, but it's all about Him!

May you walk tall today knowing that He has enriched you because you are in Him!

DAY 127

1 Corinthians 1:7

7 Therefore you do not lack any spiritual gift as you eagerly wait for our Lord Jesus Christ to be revealed.

I read verses like this throughout God's word that speak of power and the good things we have in Christ — but I do not always live in such a way that I have no lack of any spiritual gift. I don't know that I am eagerly waiting for my precious Lord to be revealed. So what am I living for?

We can look at the past things we have done in our lives and begin to regret how we have lived life. What shall I choose for today?

"Lord, today, would you keep this promise before me — the promise that I lack no spiritual gift as I wait eagerly for You to be revealed? The reality is that I may fail two minutes from now. But I pray that you would help each of us — in this moment — to live out this promise. Just for today. Amen."

DAY 128

1 Corinthians 1:8

8 He will also keep you firm to the end, so that you will be blameless on the day of our Lord Jesus Christ.

How did you do yesterday with living as though you lack no spiritual gift as you waited eagerly for the Lord to be revealed? Did you see him revealed in any way? Or was it a day that you just felt like you failed a million times over? Those days happen no matter how much you put the Word before you.

There is hope. You are in Him and He is in you. Therefore, He will keep you firm to the end. He promises that for each of His children. Today is a new day and He is working in you and me to make us blameless for the day of Christ Jesus.

"Lord Jesus, help me trust you today to keep me firm that I may be blameless before You. Amen."

DAY 129

1 Corinthians 1:9

9 God is faithful, who has called you into fellowship with his Son, Jesus Christ our Lord.

God is faithful. That sums it up. If you are facing a test, God is faithful. If you are facing teaching a class of students, God is faithful. Is there a project you are working on? Are you just enjoying another day of retirement? Maybe you are just facing an empty house. God is faithful.

But, wait! There's more! He is not some far off god or statue. No! He is faithful and He is calling you continuously into fellowship. He is with you. Our Heavenly Father wants us to talk to His Son as though He is a friend. We get to fellowship with Jesus in everything we do. The return on investment is that God is faithful!

DAY 130

1 Corinthians 1:10

10 I appeal to you, brothers and sisters, in the name of our Lord Jesus Christ, that all of you agree with one another in what you say and that there be no divisions among you, but that you be perfectly united in mind and thought.

This is a verse that convicts me. I have been told over the years that I am one who has her head on straight, but the things that go on in my thought life would reveal something very different. I know none of us are perfect in what we think because we often think in the flesh rather than in the Spirit that is in us. But Paul's appeal to the body of Christ is a strong one. He appeals to us to be unified in mind and thought. We are to agree with one another so that there is no division.

Is your mind and thought unified with those around you? Or, to take it a step further, are you loving others well no matter how they think? Can we agree to disagree and still have unity with one another?

DAY 131

1 Corinthians 1:17

17 For Christ did not send me to baptize, but to preach the gospel—not with wisdom and eloquence, lest the cross of Christ be emptied of it's power.

May God give us the grace today to share the Gospel with someone. May His power of the cross be fulfilled as we speak His truth of who He is in our lives. Yes, we should have the mindset to evangelize those who have yet to hear the truths of Christ. But, maybe you will not come in contact with a non-believer today. So, ask the Lord how He would have you share the Gospel today. Many of us have grown up in the church and know the Sunday school verses, but maybe there is someone who needs renewal through a scripture given to them.

Let the Lord speak through you. He is faithful and the power of the cross is the reason we live.

DAY 132

1 Corinthians 1:18

18 For the message of the cross is foolishness to those who are perishing, but to us who are being saved it is the power of God.

When I read this verse for the very first time, I almost fell out of my chair! What a bold statement, "but to us who are being saved it [the message of the cross] is the power of God." Oh PRAISE GOD for this sweet truth!

A challenge for you today: With every thought and every word you speak, choose to think and speak with the knowledge that the message of the cross is the power of God! How will that change your outlook for the day or even for just the next couple of minutes?

DAY 133

1 Corinthians 1:25

25 For the foolishness of God is wiser than human wisdom, and the weakness of God is stronger than human strength.

Even in his foolishness and weakness — He is better and bigger and greater and stronger! We are nothing without Him and that, my friends, is a glorious truth!

There have been a number of times when the Lord has spoken to me and I feel absolutely crazy for believing Him for His promises. In my simple human mind, I wonder, "How is this even going to come about? This is crazy!" But, there have been so many times when I think the ways of God seem foolish or I don't see how the Lord is going to come through in my weakness — and yet, God is wiser and stronger. He fulfills His promise!

This verse is a great reminder that we can depend on God in all things — no matter the outcome!

DAY 134

1 Corinthians 1:26

26 Brothers and sisters, think of what you were when you were called. Not many of you were wise by human standards; not many were influential; not many were of noble birth.

P aul's bluntness in this verse is so incredibly wonderful! He asks us to think of who we were when we were called, but then follows up by saying, "Here's who you weren't." We could look at this verse and feel pretty small and insignificant...and maybe even discouraged. Or we can choose to look back on our lives and take time to remember where the Lord has brought us from!

DAY 135

1 Corinthians 1:27-29

27 But God chose the foolish things of the world to shame the wise; God chose the weak things of the world to shame the strong. 28 God chose the lowly things of this world and the despised things—and the things that are not —to nullify the things that are, 29 so that no one may boast before him.

These are one of those "coffee cup" passages that we get so used to quoting. This passage is filled with God's choices and the reasons why he made such choices! WE may not always understand why God makes certain choices in our lives, especially if it is a choice of something that causes us to die to ourselves. But I would encourage you, today, to fall back on these verses and ask the Lord to make them fresh and awaken your heart

He is faithful in His choices! Trust Him!

DAY 136

1 Corinthians 1:30

30 It is because of him that you are in Christ Jesus, who has become for us wisdom from God—that is, our righteousness, holiness and redemption.

Now that we have thought through where the Lord has brought us from, today is a day to be thankful. It is because of the Lord that we are in Jesus Christ. May our hearts and minds be filled with thankfulness that Jesus Christ is the wisdom of God to us. He is our righteousness and holiness. And even more, He is our redemption! Our past is our past, but it doesn't have to be what defines us. Christ's redemption and the powerful message of the cross is what should be defining us!

Day 137

1 Corinthians 1:31

31 Therefore, as it is written: "Let the one who boasts boast in the Lord."

I love that Paul continuously brings us back to the Lord. It's just really not about us at all! How incredibly freeing. But the challenge lies in walking out that mindset on a daily basis. Paul tells us to boast in the Lord. He doesn't tell us to boast about ourselves and how great we are. Daily we must choose to boast in the Lord if we are to boast in anyone or anything. May God's grace be upon us to do so!

Day 138

1 Corinthians 2:3-5

3 I came to you in weakness with great fear and trembling. 4 My message and my preaching were not with wise and persuasive words, but with a demonstration of the Spirit's power, 5 so that your faith might not rest on human wisdom, but on God's power.

When we speak, do we do so with a demonstration of the Spirit's power so that others' faith will not rest on human wisdom, but on God's power?

There are a number of individuals in my own life who speak in such a way that I feel closer to and loved more by the Lord than the person sitting before me. I am so thankful to have individuals like this to walk through life with. It isn't that they are super spiritual and throwing scripture in my face, but you know they consider the Lord in their speech so that God's power may be known!

Who are those people in your life? I would encourage you to take time today and reach out to them to thank them for speaking into your life! Even the most encouraging and strong people need words of affirmation.

Day 139

1 Corinthians 2:9-10

9 However, as it is written: "What no eye has seen, what no ear has heard, and what no human mind has conceived" — 10 the things God has prepared for those who love him— these are the things God has revealed to us by his Spirit. The Spirit searches all things, even the deep things of God.

A few days ago when I sat down to write about these verses, I felt stuck and not quite sure how to wrap my mind around them. But then, in my times of prayer, I heard myself begin to pray the words, praising the Lord that He has chosen to reveal to us — through His Spirit — those things which no eye has seen, no ear has heard, and no human mind has conceived! What an incredible privilege we have as followers of the Most High God that He would look upon us and reveal His ways to us to guide and protect us as we walk through this life.

Oh! But, my sweet friends, this passage of scripture ends so intimately!!! Paul says, "The Spirit searches all things, even the deep things of God." Do you see how close the Lord desires to be with us? He loves us and wants to know us so intimately that He has chosen to give us His Spirit that searches ALL things — even the deep things of God! You really can't get any better than that!

May you rest in these truths today!

Day 140

1 Corinthians 2:11

11 For who knows a person's thoughts except their own spirit within them? In the same way no one knows the thoughts of God except the Spirit of God.

Reading verse 11 gives me a new appreciation for the spirit that is in me. I can look at this verse and be so thankful that the spirit within me is the only one that knows my thoughts. Do you have those days when you don't want to be around anyone because you know you have nothing nice to think or say about anything? Maybe I am the only one who has this issue, but on a day like that — I pray the Lord gives me the grace to be reminded of this verse.

The Lord has given us the Holy Spirit to know us and guide us. What is the Spirit telling you for today? If you are having one of those days like I described above, remember the Spirit is the one who knows your thoughts and with that, you can choose to look to the Lord and ask Him for help! He has given us the Holy Spirit as our Helper. Praise the Lord!

Day 141

1 Corinthians 4:5

5 Therefore judge nothing before the appointed time; wait until the Lord comes. He will bring to light what is hidden in darkness and will expose the motives of the heart. At that time each will receive their praise from God.

"At that time each will receive their praise from God." The ending of this verse is not what I would have expected as an ending. Paul tells us to judge nothing before the appointed time, wait for the Lord to come, because He will reveal the motives of the heart. And then we will receive praise from God?!

This puts a whole new outlook on the concept of judging others or circumstances. Sometimes we can be so quick to judge or to want change in our lives. We aren't quick to wait on the Lord until He reveals the motives of the heart. What do we miss out on when we choose to not be quick to wait on the Lord for His revelations? There are good things at the end — not just His revelations, but the praise of God!

DAY 142

1 Corinthians 4:20
20 For the kingdom of God is not a matter of
talk but of power.

What a profoundly simple statement! This verse alone is why one should believe in heaven and hell. It goes back to power. The kingdom of God is power. Why? How? Well, look at your life — no matter whether you are 18 or 80 — how have you seen the kingdom of God be a matter of power and not just talk? Give testimony of His power!

DAY 143

1 Corinthians 5:1-5

1 It is actually reported that there is sexual immorality among you, and of a kind that even pagans do not tolerate: A man is sleeping with his father's wife. And you are proud! 2 Shouldn't you rather have gone into mourning and have put out of your fellowship the man who has been doing this? 3 For my part, even though I am not physically present, I am with you in spirit. As one who is present with you in this way, I have already passed judgment in the name of our Lord Jesus on the one who has been doing this. 4 So when you are assembled and I am with you in spirit, and the power of our Lord Jesus is present, 5 hand this man over to Satan for the destruction of the flesh, so that his spirit may be saved on the day of the Lord.

We are all sinners saved by grace. I so appreciate this passage of scripture because it isn't just filled with judging someone for their sinful and sexually immoral ways. If we aren't careful, we will judge and stop there. We won't rely on the power and presence of God to help an individual.

Are we willing to follow Paul's instructions throughout this passage? Or are we too proud to put someone out of our fellowship? The first couple verses sound like they are filled with judgment and hopelessness for someone who is living in sin within a fellowship. Yes — sin is bad. It can and does rule our lives as we allow it to have power over us. If you notice, Paul tells the body of Christ that when "the power of our Lord Jesus Christ is present" — that is when they are to hand an individual over to Satan for the death of his flesh.

But, Paul doesn't stop talking there. There is a "so that", hope! Why in the power of the presence of God do we turn someone over to Satan for the death of his flesh? We do it, in His power, so that this individual's spirit "may be saved on the day of the Lord". Praise God that this whole passage points back to the power of God and His handiwork!

Don't be proud! Be willing to help those living in sin — but be sure that you are doing it in the power and presence of our Lord — otherwise it is empty!

DAY 144

1 Corinthians 5:13

13 God will judge those outside. "Expel the wicked person from among you."

This is probably a verse that you should go back and read in context because it is a rather bold statement. But, in all of this, I continue to go back to the thought that each of us will one day stand before our Heavenly Daddy and give account for our actions, our words, our thoughts — our lives. He will be the one to judge.

So with whom are you hanging out? With what are you filling your minds? What evil things or people need to be expelled from our lives? Maybe there is nothing. Or maybe it isn't necessarily evil , but I pray that each of us would take the time to allow the Lord to search us and know us and reveal to us those things which we need to expel.

[START EDITING]

Day 145

1 Corinthians 6:1-2

1 If any of you has a dispute with another, do you
dare to take it before the ungodly for judgment
instead of before the Lord's people? 2 Or do you
not know that the Lord's people will judge the
world? And if you are to judge the world, are you
not competent to judge trivial cases?

These verses got my wheels turning, not because I am questioning who I take my disputes to, but more because I wonder why anyone—as a believer—would choose to take their dispute to the ungodly for judgment. It seems obvious that this is a bad idea, until I realize that many in our court system may not be believers. Maybe I am taking these verses out of context, but it really makes me think twice about who I would take my disputes to.

As someone who is in full-time ministry, it is easy to take my disputes to a godly leader or my pastor, and that's not necessarily a bad thing. But verse 2 asks, "And if you are to judge the world, are you not competent to judge trivial cases?" I can't help but wonder if maybe there are times that I should be making my own decisions. Could it be that the Lord would have me make decisions with Him, rather than always going to man?

What foundation are you using today as you judge the trivial cases of the world or the disputes of your brothers and sisters? I pray that we would be faithful to seek the Lord's Word for direction in both the good and the bad.

DAY 146

1 Corinthians 6:3-4

3 Do you not know that we will judge angels? How much more the things of this life! 4 Therefore, if you have disputes about such matters, do you ask for a ruling from those whose way of life is scorned in the church?

Who is the Church made up of? What kind of people do you spend time with at your church? Does their life show a pouring out of God's peace and gentleness, of His Word?

Paul is very repetitive in what we read yesterday and, now, today. Which means we should pay attention! As the Lord speaks through Paul, be willing to hear from the Lord and re-evaluate, if needed, those that you allow to pour into your life as you go through trials, tribulations, and suffering.

I know that I need to hear these verses loud and clear and surround myself with men and women who will rule with the truth. And remember, ruling with truth doesn't always mean it is going to be sunshine and daisies. But, run to the Lord with the ruling and counsel you are given. He is our ultimate Judge who desires good for His children!

DAY 147

1 Corinthians 6:5-8

5 I say this to shame you. Is it possible that there is nobody among you wise enough to judge a dispute between believers? 6 But instead, one brother takes another to court—and this in front of unbelievers! The very fact that you have lawsuits among you means you have been completely defeated already. Why not rather be wronged? Why not rather be cheated? Instead, you yourselves cheat and do wrong, and you do this to your brothers and sisters.

The verbage in these verses is so incredibly powerful. I have never once been in a lawsuit or had anyone want to bring a lawsuit against me. But, in reading these verses, it makes me want to simply fall on my face before the Lord and cry out to Him for so many Christian organizations in this day and age who have had past staff bring one or more lawsuits upon them.

It is clear through these verses that lawsuits are not from the Lord. With this scripture in mind, would you take time today and pray for many believers who have come against Christian ministries within our own country and are trying to take them down through lawsuits?

Here are a couple of ways you can pray specifically:

1. Believers who feel it is the right and godly thing to bring a lawsuit against a Christian organization.

2. The Lord would sustain the leadership and staff of these different organizations as they go through the process of lawsuits.

3. Godly judges who will rule objectively and look at all the facts presented before them.

4. Changed hearts that we, as believers, would live by the truth of God's Word.

DAY 148

1 Corinthians 6:9-10

9 Or do you not know that wrongdoers will not inherit the kingdom of God? Do not be deceived: Neither the sexually immoral nor idolaters nor adulterers nor men who have sex with men 10 nor thieves nor the greedy nor drunkards nor slanderers nor swindlers will inherit the kingdom of God. And that is what some of you were.

Excuse me while I pick my jaw up off the floor from the bluntness of Paul! These verses are so great! I read this list above of the "types" of wrong doers who will not inherit the Kingdom of God and, wow! Does that ever weed out so many people?!?

But there is redemption through our Heavenly Daddy. As Paul writes, "And that is what some of you were." Don't forget where you came from! Trust in the beautiful redemption of Jesus on the cross!

Day 149

1 Corinthians 6:11

11 But you were washed, you were sanctified, you were justified in the name of the Lord Jesus Christ and by the Spirit of our God.

Praise the Lord! What a wonderful and uplifting promise to hold onto for today! This is worth reading many times over. It is so rich in what the Lord Jesus Christ has done for us as His children. We are not alone. The even greater part of this is that He has washed, sanctified, and justified each of us individually in His name and by the Spirit of our God!

This verse makes my heart smile and I hope it does the same for you!

Day 150

1 Corinthians 6:13-14

13 You say, "Food for the stomach and the stomach for food, and God will destroy them both." 14 The body, however, is not meant for sexual immorality but for the Lord, and the Lord for the body. By his power God raised the Lord from the dead, and he will raise us also.

This passage speaks volumes. It can be taken different ways, the first one being that you just skip over it because it has the words "sexual immorality" in it and, well, that can be an uncomfortable subject. The second way is to read it word for word and allow God to saturate your Spirit with His truth.

"The body, however, is not meant for sexual immorality but for the Lord, and the Lord for the body."

It is what it is and there is really no way around it. This is a challenging truth of God's Word which we must hold tightly to in this day and age. But with the bluntness of God's Word also comes hope! The redemption is in the last few words, "he will raise us also." Oh, how glorious!

DAY 151

1 Corinthians 6:15-17

15 Do you not know that your bodies are members of Christ himself? Shall I then take the members of Christ and unite them with a prostitute? Never! 16 Do you not know that he who unites himself with a prostitute is one with her in body? For it is said, "The two will become one flesh." But whoever is united with the Lord is one with him in spirit.

Where are our priorities? Most of you who are reading this have never united yourself with a prostitute. Let's be honest. Yet, this passage has powerful wording that speaks of two becoming one flesh. Maybe you don't have that personal connection of two becoming one in a sexually immoral way.

But look at your life. What do you hold in high esteem? Can you read the last sentence of this passage, "But whoever is united with the Lord is one with him in spirit", and know that this is true in your life?

Am I, [insert your name], united with the Lord? This just brings the reality of how close God wants to be with each of us to a whole new level.

DAY 152

1 Corinthians 6:18

18 Flee from sexual immorality. All other sins a person commits are outside the body, but whoever sins sexually, sins against their own body.

Woah! Day after day, this subject of sexual immorality continues to come up. Yes! We must pay attention! God is speaking so clearly through Paul and this is not a subject that we can let slide. He calls us to flee from it! And then he goes and makes it really personal by saying that if we sin sexually, then we are sinning against our own selves.

You know, the more scripture I come across about sexual immorality, the more I realize how serious God is! This isn't something to mess with by any means. It is personal. Something we must, individually, take before the Lord and be open to the things He wants to reveal in us.

Maybe you have never sinned sexually. That doesn't mean this verse can't apply to you in some way. Maybe your prayer could be, "Lord, help me to continue to be faithful and not give in to any sexual sins."

If you are someone who has faced such sins, remember the Lord redeems, just as we read the other day. He will raise you up, so take time to wrestle this through with the Lord. He is waiting and will bend His ear towards you—for you are His child!

167

DAY 153

1 Corinthians 6:19-20

19 Do you not know that your bodies are temples of the Holy Spirit, who is in you, whom you have received from God? You are not your own; 20 you were bought at a price. Therefore honor God with your bodies.

This is truly a beautiful passage of truth. I love that our bodies are a temple of the Holy Spirit! Just think about that: God created our very beings, our bodies, to be a temple of part of the Trinity! I don't know about you, but I certainly don't think of my body in that way when I look in the mirror.

The world tells us to paint our faces with make-up or wear this pair of jeans to look skinnier or cut our hair a certain way so that we will look beautiful. But, brothers and sisters, our Almighty Heavenly Father — the Creator of Heaven and Earth — has created our individual bodies to be a TEMPLE of the Holy Spirit!

If that doesn't make you feel washed and pure, I don't know what will! God is so good to us in His unfailing love and creating each of us for His glory!

"Therefore honor God with your bodies."

DAY 154

2 Corinthians 1:3-4

3 Praise be to the God and Father of our Lord Jesus Christ, the Father of compassion and the God of all comfort, who comforts us 4 in all our troubles, so that we can comfort those in any trouble with the comfort we ourselves receive from God.

Every morning, my Uncle Roy walked 4 to 5 miles as he talked with the Lord on behalf of each of our family members. On September 21, 2018, he was crossing the street near his apartment when a pick-up truck came around the corner and hit him, putting him in the Critical Care Unit and long recovery.

A few weeks after he had been hit, the Lord brought me across verses 3 & 4 in my reading through the Bible. These are verses I have read several times, but this time it struck me deeper as the Lord brought my Uncle Roy and Aunt Anette to mind. They were smack-dab in the middle of a difficult and painful situation. My uncle will know physical suffering in a whole new light. But the Lord is Sovereign.

Our God — the Lord Jesus Christ — is the Father of compassion and the God of comfort. You see, though, He is not the God of some comfort based on how He feels towards one of His children. No — He is the God of ALL comfort! And He was so incredibly present with my Uncle Roy and Aunt Anette, bringing them ALL the comfort they needed for their troubles SO THAT they would be able to comfort others who face trouble. Oh, it just gives me chills to think about how much the Lord loves His precious saints that He would entrust my uncle and aunt with such a painful situation so that they can be used by Him to comfort others.

And that is the testimony that flows from both of them — no matter the pain, the good days, the bad days, or the long road ahead. The Lord is near!

DAY 155

2 Corinthians 1:5

5 For just as we share abundantly in the sufferings of Christ, so also our comfort abounds through Christ.

There is no negativity in this verse. My sweet friend, we have been chosen to share ABUNDANTLY in the sufferings of Christ!!! I know I may sound a little crazy to be so excited by this verse, but THIS is the truth of God that our precious lives represent! This verse isn't saying that we will suffer alone. It's just the opposite. We get to share in the sufferings of Christ.

On top of the abundant sharing of suffering, our comfort abounds. It doesn't abound through one another or our own selves. Our comfort ABOUNDS THROUGH Christ! I can't get enough of this. I just want to breathe it in deeply and then get up and dance with joy because TODAY I get to share abundantly in the sufferings of Christ AND my comfort will ABOUND through Christ!

DAY 156

2 Corinthians 1:7

7 And our hope for you is firm, because we know
that just as you share in our sufferings, so also
you share in our comfort.

Praise the Lord! I challenge you, today, to look for ways the
Lord wants you to share in others' sufferings and comfort.
What magnificent things is the Lord going to do through you as
you relate to others?

DAY 157

2 Corinthians 1:8

8 We do not want you to be uninformed, brothers and sisters, about the troubles we experienced in the province of Asia. We were under great pressure, far beyond our ability to endure, so that we despaired of life itself.

There are many brothers and sisters throughout Asia that are sharing the love of Christ with communities. They are facing persecution and suffering that is "beyond their ability to endure". So let us take a few moments today to pray for them as they faithfully follow the Lord in the calling He has given them.

We can pray for:

1. Strength

2. Endurance

3. Love for their persecutors

4. Clear discernment in every situation they are in

Ask the Lord to lead you as you pray for our brothers and sisters. He knows their situations and knows them by name.

Day 158

2 Corinthians 1:9

9 Indeed, we felt we had received the sentence of death. But this happened that we might not rely on ourselves but on God, who raises the dead.

Is there a "sentence of death" you felt you received in the past? Maybe a relational issue or sin struggle you have been holding onto? Today is the day to seek Him to help you let go.

Because you are human and have emotions that help you to hold onto the past, you can't learn to let go in your own strength. The last part of verse 9 says, "But this happened that we might not rely on ourselves but on God…" We don't have to go at this alone! Rely on the Lord to walk you through whatever it is you need to let go of. Be patient and know that the Lord's timing is perfect.

DAY 159

2 Corinthians 1:10-11

10 He has delivered us from such a deadly peril, and he will deliver us again. On him we have set our hope that he will continue to deliver us, 11 as you help us by your prayers. Then many will give thanks on our behalf for the gracious favor granted us in answer to the prayers of many.

I am writing this devotional at the end of a week that was rather difficult physically, emotionally, and mentally. I don't like when weeks like this come because I am always caught off guard. However, the Lord gives us the "power tools" we need through His Word.

Verse 10 says, "He has delivered us…he will deliver us again… On him we have set our hope that he will continue to deliver us…" This deliverance from the Lord is a past, present, and future action. Great! But what about those days when things are just really hard and you don't know how to battle through it on your own? Those days when you may know that this promise of deliverance is true, but you just can't get it to stick.

Thank goodness Paul doesn't stop there. He ends the thought by saying, "…as you help us by your prayer." We can ask others to pray for us. If you don't have a mentor or a couple close people in your life that you can actively ask to pray for you, I encourage you to find those people. Let others battle with you! We aren't called to go through this life alone — God calls us into community. You see that all throughout scripture. Through asking for prayer from others, we give them the opportunity to give thanks on our behalf as the Lord answers the prayers of many!

Day 160

2 Corinthians 2:5-11

5 If anyone has caused grief, he has not so much grieved me as he has grieved all of you to some extent—not to put it too severely. 6 The punishment inflicted on him by the majority is sufficient. 7 Now instead, you ought to forgive and comfort him, so that he will not be overwhelmed by excessive sorrow. 8 I urge you, therefore, to reaffirm your love for him. 9 Another reason I wrote you was to see if you would stand the test and be obedient in everything. 10 Anyone you forgive, I also forgive. And what I have forgiven— if there was anything to forgive—I have forgiven in the sight of Christ for your sake, 11 in order that Satan might not outwit us. For we are not unaware of his schemes.

Paul is saying we are to forgive and comfort those who have grieved us…in order to reaffirm our love for them. Wow! How many people have grieved me over the years and because I didn't choose to forgive and comfort, my love was not reaffirmed for them?

Paul then goes a step further and says he forgives them in the sight of Christ for our sake. How much of these verses are more for our benefit than for the one who has grieved us? Yes, there are actions for us to take to forgive and comfort, but it benefits us in reaffirming a deep love for them that really can only come from Christ.

To me, Paul is saying that he is forgiving them in the sight of Christ — he isn't holding what they did against them — so we shouldn't either. We are called to forgive and comfort. Point blank. Forgive. Forgive. Forgive.

DAY 161

Genesis 1:26

26 Then God said, "Let us make mankind in our image, in our likeness, so that they may rule over the fish in the sea and the birds in the sky, over the livestock and all the wild animals, and over all the creatures that move along the ground."

I never realized that this verse's reference to making "mankind" is a totally separate reference from when God created Adam. I love that God is so repetitive and detailed. He is patient with us when we don't catch on to something the first time. He is always willing to bring that same concept up again later in our story with a different twist. Sometimes He provides us with the big picture, but waits to give us the details.

I feel like that is what He did with this verse. He gives us the big picture of "Let us make mankind…" so they can do this, this, and this. But then later on in the story, He describes how He made Adam and Eve.

Watch for the details today, even if you are a "big picture" kind of thinker. If you are a "detailed brain" person, like me, may God give us the grace to look at the "big picture". He has created us all in a certain way, but may we take the time to look at other viewpoints as well.

DAY 162

Genesis 2:15-17

15 The Lord God took the man and put him in the Garden of Eden to work it and take care of it. 16 And the Lord God commanded the man, "You are free to eat from any tree in the garden; 17 but you must not eat from the tree of the knowledge of good and evil, for when you eat from it you will certainly die."

Question: If you were in the Garden of Eden — naked and unashamed — and you knew that everything before you was good, why would you ever want to know the difference between good and evil?

DAY 163

Ephesians 4:22

22 You were taught, with regard to your former way of life, to put off your old self, which is being corrupted by its deceitful desires...

During my quiet time one morning, I was reading the latter part of Ephesians Chapter 4, which is titled, "Instructions for Christian Living". I must say, some of these verses convict me as I start my day and think back on the last several days of my life. So, I thought I would take a few days here and see what the Lord wants to teach us through some of these verses.

Sometimes as I read a verse like Ephesians 4:22, it seems so unattainable to me. Really, though, it is a simple and conscious daily decision to "put off your old self". Some days, those desires deceive us more than others. But it is a choice. What are these desires that are deceiving you?

Did I just touch a raw nerve? If so, I hope you will take it to the Lord and trust Him to bring you through it as He so faithfully does when we seek Him first!

DAY 164

Ephesians 4:23

23 to be made new in the attitude of your minds...

O h, this is a good verse! What is the attitude of my mind today? Is it negative? Positive? Hopeful? Frustrated? What is the attitude of your mind today? Whatever it may be, let's take a step back in this moment and ask the Lord to make us new in the attitude of our minds! In order to do this, we have to rely on the Lord's truth and promises.

DAY 165

Ephesians 4:24
24 and to put on the new self, created to be like
God in true righteousness and holiness.

Yesterday we talked about being made new in the attitude of our minds. Was that helpful? Do you feel different today? As we are made new in our minds, it becomes so much easier to put the new self on. From the beginning of time, God created us to be like Him.

Verse 24 says, "in true righteousness and holiness".
Deep breath.
True righteousness.
And holiness.

Thank you, Lord, for your many promises.

DAY 166

Ephesians 4:25
25 Therefore each of you must put off falsehood and speak truthfully to your neighbor, for we are all members of one body.

I so often speak and don't think about what is actually coming out of my mouth until after the fact. I think that is why this verse convicts me. Maybe it isn't that I am speaking falsely, but I could definitely watch more intently what comes from my mouth. Is it truthful? Is it uplifting? We are all members of one body, and we are called to build each other up. So let's do that today.

If you want to take it a step further, I would encourage you to write down how you spoke truthfully to someone today. OR, maybe, how you didn't. This will show us where we need to ask the Lord to help us. It may not be a fun lesson to learn, but it will be good in the end.

DAY 167

Ephesians 4:26-27

26 "In your anger do not sin": Do not let the sun go down while you are still angry, 27 and do not give the devil a foothold.

L et me ask you: As a child (or maybe as an adult), how many times did you have verse 26 quoted to you? Did it make you feel all warm and fuzzy inside? Or, were you human, and it just made you more angry?

It's okay to admit it made you more angry. I know it did for me. That's right — none of us are perfect!

But then verse 27 says, "and do not give the devil a foothold." So, if we don't go to bed angry, then the devil has no room for a foothold, right?

When someone quotes verse 26 to you, just remember the next verse. If you are angry as the sun goes down, that means the enemy has a foothold. This doesn't mean that you hold onto your anger until the last possible second. No, it means you ask the Lord to help you put off that anger.

We have a victory already. There is no room for the devil's foot!

DAY 168

Genesis 3:16

16 To the woman he said, "I will make your pains in childbearing very severe; with painful labor you will give birth to children. Your desire will be for your husband, and he will rule over you."

The Lord never misses a beat. There is truly something in the Bible for every situation. I don't know that this is the verse I would want put before me as I am giving birth to a child — probably not the most encouraging piece of God's Word!

Although the first part, as it talks about pain, sounds rather awful — God still brings beauty in the midst of the pain. He says, "Your desire will be for your husband, and he will rule over you." This sentence speaks of what marriage is truly to be. Our desire for the Bridegroom and for Him to rule over us.

The Lord has so intimately intertwined beauty and pain as He speaks of His relationship with us and of making us one with Him!

DAY 169

Galatians 1:10

10 Am I now trying to win the approval of human beings, or of God? Or am I trying to please people? If I were still trying to please people, I would not be a servant of Christ.

A re you a people pleaser? Yes — it is a blunt question, and yet, it is one I have to ask myself often. I love how Paul so plainly writes out his question: "Am I now trying to win the approval of human beings, or of God?" You know, you could end the verse right there and call it a day. You could just sit and take in those questions alone and, probably, be rather content in your thought life trying to figure it all out.

But we can't just stop there... because people pleasing means not serving Christ. So we also have to ask – "which would I rather do?"

So it comes down to this: People pleasing equals not being a servant of Christ.

Which would you rather be?

Day 170

Genesis 7:17-20

17 For forty days the flood kept coming on the earth, and as the waters increased they lifted the ark high above the earth. 18 The waters rose and increased greatly on the earth, and the ark floated on the surface of the water. 19 They rose greatly on the earth, and all the high mountains under the entire heavens were covered. 20 The waters rose and covered the mountains to a depth of more than fifteen cubits.

Can we just take a moment and focus on the fact that the story of Noah and the Ark is written in the early chapters of the Bible?! I know there is a lot of time that passed, but it seems crazy that chapter 6 is the start of the flood to wipe out creation!

But as I read chapter 7, verses 17-21, I kept thinking about those times I have faced mountain-top experiences, only to have the flood waters overtake the mountain.

Today, I would encourage you to go back and read chapter 6-7:20. Write down ways that God prepared Noah and his family for the flood waters that overtook the mountains. I would be interested to hear what the Lord reveals to you!

Day 171

Genesis 7:21-23

21 Every liviZng thing that moved on land perished—birds, livestock, wild animals, all the creatures that swarm over the earth, and all mankind. 22 Everything on dry land that had the breath of life in its nostrils died. 23 Every living thing on the face of the earth was wiped out; people and animals and the creatures that move along the ground and the birds were wiped from the earth. Only Noah was left, and those with him in the ark.

If you read these verses very carefully, you will notice they state three different times that the Lord wiped out everything on the face of the earth. But verse 23 ends with hope. Yes, the Lord wiped out the earth, yet Noah, and those with him in the ark, were left.

Trauma. Rain. Death. Loss. Grieving. Loneliness. Isolation. We could look at these verses and think, "How horrible! How could the Lord do this to His creation?" I'm not sure, though, that that is how the Lord wants us to see these verses. So, he put a sentence of hope at the end. He left Noah on the ark and those with him.

Here's the way I see this: the Lord has handpicked each one of us. We get to face trials and see trauma right outside the windows of our arks (i.e. our lives), but we aren't alone. We have community.

Maybe community isn't always evident, but it is there. There were two of every kind of animal, Noah's family, and Noah. The Lord will bring restoration and redemption! Be patient!

DAY 172

Deuteronomy 30:14
14 No, the word is very near you; it is in your mouth and in your heart so you may obey it.

Is this the way I live my life? Is this the way you live your life? I know that we can't change the past, let alone even the last minute of the thoughts that went through our hearts and minds, but as we each move forward today — may we remember this verse. My prayer is that we would live every minute knowing that the Word of God is near.

This is one of those verses that I would just love to have always before me. At the same time, it is probably the first one I will forget as I start into the business of my day.

Do you have someone in your life that could keep you accountable to this verse? Yes, I know it will be a challenge. But it is also to be a privilege to carry God's Word in our mouths and hearts that we would obey it.

Cross reference to Luke 6:45, "Out of the heart the mouth speaks."

Day 173

Genesis 1:5-8

5 God called the light "day," and the darkness he called "night." And there was evening, and there was morning—the first day.

6 And God said, "Let there be a vault between the waters to separate water from water." 7 So God made the vault and separated the water under the vault from the water above it. And it was so. 8 God called the vault "sky." And there was evening, and there was morning—the second day.

Could you imagine if we referred to the sky as the vault? *"Look how blue the vault is!"*

Just think about it. It gives a whole new meaning to what the Lord created the sky to hold and separate!

DAY 174

Genesis 2:7

7 Then the Lord God formed a man from the dust of the ground and breathed into his nostrils the breath of life, and the man became a living being.

I t would be so easy to pass by this verse and think, "Oh that's cool. God created man." But God breathed into Adam's nostrils to give him the breath of life. Just think about that for a moment. What would it mean to have God breathe into YOUR nostrils to give you the breath of life? God would have to be awfully close to your face to breathe into your nostrils.

I don't know about you, but this verse makes me feel so deeply loved by God! The same God who is the Creator of the Universe, saw fit to create man and breathe life into him. He has created you just as He created Adam — knowing how we would fail Him. What an unconditionally loving God we belong to!!!

DAY 175

Genesis 2:21

21 So the Lord God caused the man to fall into a deep sleep; and while he was sleeping, he took one of the man's ribs and then closed up the place with flesh.

God was the first anesthesiologist! This is encouraging to know that God can understand firsthand how important anesthesiology is in the midst of surgery. The next time you have surgery or know of someone who is having surgery, may you remember this verse and pray for that anesthesiologist, that the Lord would guide him or her as they do their part.

Remember, God totally gets it. He understands how the body functions because He created it! We can fear the Lord in this rather than fearing what may or may not go wrong with anesthesia.

DAY 176

Leviticus 3:16
16 The priest shall burn them on the altar as a food offering, a pleasing aroma. All the fat is the Lord's.

If today's devotional seems random, it's because it is. I was recently listening to a podcast about getting healthy, and one of the hosts brought up this verse, rather humorously, that says, "...All the fat is the Lord's." Although, that may be slightly out of context in light of eating healthy or losing weight, it is an encouraging sentence!

You are getting very close to the half way point of this devotional. Congratulations! You have made it this far and I do hope the Lord is teaching you a lot! It is so easy to rush through our devotional times, but not really remember what we have read or heard from the Lord. My challenge to you today is this: Don't just continue to read through this devotional in order to check off "Quiet Time" on your list, but rather, find ways to help you remember what the Lord is teaching you. For instance, I am sure I have read Leviticus chapter 3 many times, but because it is about how offerings should be handled, I just gloss over the words. But, because of the podcast and remembering that, "All the fat is the Lord's", it drives me to want to read the full context of the chapter and see what else the Lord might want to show me.

The Lord is faithful. You just have to look up and remember His faithfulness!

Day 177

Genesis 3:12-13

12 The man said, "The woman you put here with me—she gave me some fruit from the tree, and I ate it."

13 Then the Lord God said to the woman, "What is this you have done?"

The woman said, "The serpent deceived me, and I ate."

Talk about being thrown under the bus! Although it may be true that Eve gave Adam the fruit and that the serpent deceived Eve, how quickly Adam and Eve refused to take responsibility for their actions.

It is so much easier, in our fallen nature, to blame others rather than admit that we, ourselves, are in the wrong. Relational issues started early in this world.

The Lord is a God of compassion and forgiveness, so the question arises in my mind: How intimately did Adam and Eve know God's character?

I ask this question, but even in that, I am blaming them. If Adam and Eve knew God's character, then they should have been able to own up and admit their faults, knowing that God is a compassionate and forgiving God. We, too, have this knowledge. And yet we are also quick to not take responsibility for our actions.

My prayer for myself and you today: *Daddy, would you please graciously bring these verses to mind when we, as your created ones, want to blame those around us? May we learn how to humble ourselves in Your presence! In Your Name, Amen.*

DAY 178

Genesis 4:6-7

6 Then the Lord said to Cain, "Why are you angry? Why is your face downcast? 7 If you do what is right, will you not be accepted? But if you do not do what is right, sin is crouching at your door; it desires to have you, but you must rule over it."

These verses give clear evidence that we are in a battle. The Lord speaks so plainly to Cain. As I read this short conversation, I can clearly see how I need the Lord's bluntness like this in my own life.

I imagine needing to hear something along these lines from the Lord: "Shareen, why is your face downcast? It's so obvious. Do what is right and you will be accepted. But if you don't do what is right, sin is right there. It's waiting — even crouching. It desires to have you! Oh, but wait…one other thing, my dear child: you must rule over it!"

My friends, we can rule over sin. The Lord empowers us to do so!

Day 179

Genesis 4:9

9 Then the Lord said to Cain, "Where is your brother Abel?"

"I don't know," he replied. "Am I my brother's keeper?"

God asks the questions He already knows the answers to.

Reading this verse makes me think of parenting. I am not a parent, but I have definitely been in the kid's position of doing something wrong and having my parent call me out on it. In situations like this, we—as kids—always own up, right?

If you are human…you should have answered "no" to that question! We do what Cain did and find a way to not take responsibility for our actions.

Of course, Cain's actions were extreme, since he committed murder! But I love that God calls him out on it. Just like our parents, our Heavenly Daddy gives us opportunity to come clean and experience redemption. If we would only take it!

Day 180

Genesis 4:15-16

15 But the Lord said to him, "Not so; anyone who kills Cain will suffer vengeance seven times over." Then the Lord put a mark on Cain so that no one who found him would kill him. 16 So Cain went out from the Lord's presence and lived in the land of Nod, east of Eden.

Although God removed Cain from His presence, He still put a mark on Cain to protect him from anyone killing him.

God is our Protector and there is just no way around this. May we never forget His protection.

Day 181

Genesis 6:6

6 The Lord regretted that he had made human beings on the earth, and his heart was deeply troubled.

God regretted that He had made humans...His heart was greatly troubled.

I truly believe that there are some passages of scripture that aren't meant to be understood by the human mind. Yet, they are there that we may understand God's character.

I am not sure I want to understand the depth of pain God felt as He looked at the wickedness of His creation. He knows pain, and that is enough for me as I walk through life and the unjustness of this world.

DAY 182

Genesis 6:9

9 This is the account of Noah and his family.

Noah was a righteous man, blameless among the people of his time, and he walked faithfully with God.

Noah was blameless before the people and walked faithfully with God. Those would be some big shoes to fill.

What does it mean to you to walk faithfully with God? It seems like there should be a pretty standard Christian answer to this question. Then again, I don't know how to wrap my mind around this as I face deep hurts or issues in my life.

Lord, would you show me what it means to walk faithfully with You?

DAY 183

Genesis 8:22

22 "As long as the earth endures,

seedtime and harvest,

cold and heat,

summer and winter,

day and night

will never cease."

The mark of the four seasons.

What is your favorite season of the year? Why? Spend some time today thanking the Lord for your favorite season!

Day 184

Genesis 13:14

14 The Lord said to Abram after Lot had parted from him, "Look around from where you are, to the north and south, to the east and west.

This verse picks up with how God is blessing Abram with land and so many offspring that cannot be counted. How is God blessing you?

Day 185

Genesis 15:1
15 After this, the word of the Lord came to
Abram in a vision:
"Do not be afraid, Abram.
I am your shield,
your very great reward."

What an awesome promise! This verse speaks boldly of an ability to conquer anything that is placed before me because I am a child of the Most High! The challenge comes in remembering and actively living it out.

Today we get to carry this promise that He is our shield and exceedingly great reward!

DAY 186

Genesis 16:1-6

16 Now Sarai, Abram's wife, had borne him no children. But she had an Egyptian slave named Hagar; 2 so she said to Abram, "The Lord has kept me from having children. Go, sleep with my slave; perhaps I can build a family through her." Abram agreed to what Sarai said. 3 So after Abram had been living in Canaan ten years, Sarai his wife took her Egyptian slave Hagar and gave her to her husband to be his wife. 4 He slept with Hagar, and she conceived.

When she knew she was pregnant, she began to despise her mistress. 5 Then Sarai said to Abram, "You are responsible for the wrong I am suffering. I put my slave in your arms, and now that she knows she is pregnant, she despises me. May the Lord judge between you and me."

6 "Your slave is in your hands," Abram said. "Do with her whatever you think best." Then Sarai mistreated Hagar; so she fled from her.

W hy did Abram decide to follow and agree to Sarai's plan to sleep with Hagar? I think it is so crazy that Abram followed Sarai's plan even though God had already promised him a son. Sarai wore the pants!

As women, we must be careful to not overstep the boundaries God has established for us. To put it bluntly, let the man lead! And if he isn't leading well or in a godly manner, then be woman enough to run to the Lord and pray for that particular man, because God has created us to be helpers! This applies to single women just as much as it does to married women. Learn to appreciate the role God has created us for.

And men, pray for the women that God has given you to lead, that we would follow you in the strength of the Lord. It is just as challenging to follow you as it is for you to lead us!

DAY 187

Genesis 16:7-8

7 The angel of the Lord found Hagar near a spring in the desert; it was the spring that is beside the road to Shur. 8 And he said, "Hagar, slave of Sarai, where have you come from, and where are you going?"

The angel of the Lord called her by name and asked her, "Where have you come from and where are you going?"

I appreciate the intimacy of conversation throughout the Bible, whether that is from God or His angels. It is proof that we are known inside and out. We can keep running, but the Lord is always there with His angels to draw us back!

Sometimes when I want to run from an issue in my life or feel I want to hide from the Lord, I think about the Lord asking me a question such as the one He asked Hagar.

Day 188

Genesis 17:1-2

1 When Abram was ninety-nine years old, the Lord appeared to him and said, "I am God Almighty; walk before me faithfully and be blameless. 2 Then I will make my covenant between me and you and will greatly increase your numbers."

The Lord totally brought restoration to Abraham even though he had gone ahead with Sarai's plan. God redeems the stupid! We really are like "dumb" sheep who have gone astray!

DAY 189

Genesis 18:9-15

9 "Where is your wife Sarah?" they asked him. "There, in the tent," he said.

10 Then one of them said, "I will surely return to you about this time next year, and Sarah your wife will have a son."

Now Sarah was listening at the entrance to the tent, which was behind him. 11 Abraham and Sarah were already very old, and Sarah was past the age of childbearing. 12 So Sarah laughed to herself as she thought, "After I am worn out and my lord is old, will I now have this pleasure?"

13 Then the Lord said to Abraham, "Why did Sarah laugh and say, 'Will I really have a child, now that I am old?' 14 Is anything too hard for the Lord? I will return to you at the appointed time next year, and Sarah will have a son."

15 Sarah was afraid, so she lied and said, "I did not laugh."

But he said, "Yes, you did laugh."

Sarah really amazes me! She doesn't seem to have much faith and she laughed at God's plan for her to have a baby in her old age. She seems to be one who thinks more on her circumstances than the power of God.

If we are being honest with ourselves, maybe we should think about the times we have laughed at the plans of God. When I was away from full-time ministry, there were many instances where I wanted to laugh at the plans of God because all my circumstances were pointing away from what He was telling me was going to happen.

I am inspired by the realness of the conversations the Lord has with Abraham and Sarah throughout this passage. She laughs. The Lord calls her out on it. She tries to act as though she didn't laugh. And yet, the Lord knows us so intimately.

No matter what you may be going through in life or even just today, remember that the Lord created you and He is outside of time. Our circumstances will inevitably change and plans we see physically in front of us may appear to be directing us in another direction, but the Lord redeems.

His timing is perfect. Just wait. Stand firm. Nothing is too hard for the Lord!

Day 190

Genesis 18:14

14 Is anything too hard for the Lord? I will return to you at the appointed time next year, and Sarah will have a son."

I s anything too hard for the Lord?

I don't know about you, but I like my plans, boxes, check lists, and organization. I fear the unknown. Can you relate?

In the midst of that fear though, I forget who the Lord is. I forget to ask myself, "Is anything too hard for the Lord?"

The Lord often has to remind me that He is the One who created this "planner" brain in me. But, He didn't create me this way so I could just rely on my own strength and plans. No, he created me this way and then provided thousands of promises to show me how to depend on him.

Remember where the Lord has brought you from. Rest in the hope and faith that there is NOTHING too hard for the Lord!!!

Day 191

Genesis 18:26-33

26 The Lord said, "If I find fifty righteous people in the city of Sodom, I will spare the whole place for their sake."

27 Then Abraham spoke up again: "Now that I have been so bold as to speak to the Lord, though I am nothing but dust and ashes, 28 what if the number of the righteous is five less than fifty? Will you destroy the whole city for lack of five people?"

"If I find forty-five there," he said, "I will not destroy it."

29 Once again he spoke to him, "What if only forty are found there?"

He said, "For the sake of forty, I will not do it."

30 Then he said, "May the Lord not be angry, but let me speak. What if only thirty can be found there?"

He answered, "I will not do it if I find thirty there."

31 Abraham said, "Now that I have been so bold as to speak to the Lord, what if only twenty can be found there?"

He said, "For the sake of twenty, I will not destroy it."

32 Then he said, "May the Lord not be angry, but
let me speak just once more. What if only ten can
be found there?"
He answered, "For the sake of ten, I will not
destroy it."
33 When the Lord had finished speaking with
Abraham, he left, and Abraham returned home.
"What if this…?"
"What if that…?"
"What if? What if? What if, Lord?"

The Lord is truly patient to wait and bring reassurance to
Abraham's "what if" questions throughout this passage of
scripture. I believe it is God's grace that he put this particular passage in scripture because it proves, once again, that there is a verse
or verses for everything we face in life. And the Lord will not fail
us. He will be patient when we are weak in faith.

When you are asking, "What if?", always remember to stop
and listen for His voice. He is right before you and all around you
waiting to answer. He is there to remind you that He has a solution
for everything and we need not worry.

For their sake. No matter how many are found. He will not
destroy. Trust in Him.

DAY 192

Genesis 20:3

3 But God came to Abimelek in a dream one night and said to him, "You are as good as dead because of the woman you have taken; she is a married woman."

I can't imagine what it would be like for Abimelek to have God appear to him and say, "You are as good as dead." There are so many emotions that are running around in my head when I begin to try and put myself in Abimelek's place. I feel like those words from the Lord would stick so deeply in my soul. That would definitely be a direct way to get my attention to call me out on my sin!

Is there something you are facing today or in this week that you need the Lord to wake you up on and get your attention? Or could you thank the Lord for a time in the past when he got your attention and changed you?

DAY 193

Genesis 20:4-7

4 Now Abimelek had not gone near her, so he said, "Lord, will you destroy an innocent nation? 5 Did he not say to me, 'She is my sister,' and didn't she also say, 'He is my brother'? I have done this with a clear conscience and clean hands."

6 Then God said to him in the dream, "Yes, I know you did this with a clear conscience, and so I have kept you from sinning against me. That is why I did not let you touch her. 7 Now return the man's wife, for he is a prophet, and he will pray for you and you will live. But if you do not return her, you may be sure that you and all who belong to you will die."

What a beautiful conversation between Abimelek and God. It is so down to earth and direct. There is no beating around the bush between the two of them.

DAY 194

Genesis 24:40

40 "He replied, 'The Lord, before whom I have walked faithfully, will send his angel with you and make your journey a success, so that you can get a wife for my son from my own clan and from my father's family....'"

Because Abraham walked faithfully with his God, the Lord sent his angels with the servant and made his journey successful. Thank you Lord!

DAY 195

Genesis 24:45
45 "Before I finished praying in my heart, Rebekah came out, with her jar on her shoulder. She went down to the spring and drew water, and I said to her, 'Please give me a drink.'..."

Before the servant finished praying, the Lord was already answering his prayer.

Because prayer is the foundation of GFA World, it would be easy to forget that: a.) the expectancy should be for the Lord to answer and b.) he might even do it before they're done praying.

Today, I challenge myself, and you as well, to pray with expectancy that the Lord will answer our requests before we are done praying. Now, I say that with an understanding that the Lord doesn't always answer our prayers in the exact way we verbalize our request to him. I encourage you to wait. Be still. Stand firm and listen for what He is saying to you. If you sense a silence, be willing to be OK with the silence. He is there. Just wait.

DAY 196

Genesis 24:50

50 Laban and Bethuel answered, "This is from the Lord; we can say nothing to you one way or the other...."

"This is from the Lord, we can say nothing to you one way or the other."

This verse makes me smile and be at peace. God is faithful and His people are in agreement with what He has done!

Be bold today. Give testimony to someone around you about something the Lord is teaching you or that He has done.

DAY 197

Genesis 25:23

23 The Lord said to her,

"Two nations are in your womb,

and two peoples from within you will be
separated;

one people will be stronger than the other,

and the older will serve the younger."

Have you ever used the last sentence in this
verse on your older sibling when you are trying
to prove that they should do something for you?

"...and the older will serve the younger."

I am not sure that is why the Lord put that sentence as part of this
promise, but I know I have thought this towards my siblings or
others who are older than me. True confession.

What can we learn from this verse? The Lord has a plan for
each of us, no matter whether we are young or old. We are called
to serve one another.

Day 198

Genesis 26:6-11

6 So Isaac stayed in Gerar.

7 When the men of that place asked him about his wife, he said, "She is my sister," because he was afraid to say, "She is my wife." He thought, "The men of this place might kill me on account of Rebekah, because she is beautiful."

8 When Isaac had been there a long time, Abimelek king of the Philistines looked down from a window and saw Isaac caressing his wife Rebekah. 9 So Abimelek summoned Isaac and said, "She is really your wife! Why did you say, 'She is my sister'?"

Isaac answered him, "Because I thought I might lose my life on account of her."

10 Then Abimelek said, "What is this you have done to us? One of the men might well have slept with your wife, and you would have brought guilt upon us."

11 So Abimelek gave orders to all the people: "Anyone who harms this man or his wife shall surely be put to death."

Why did Issac lie and say Rebekah was his sister? He did the same thing Abraham did with Sarah.

It is hard to know what should be said about Issac's action of lying about who Rebekah was to him. The one thing that comes to mind is that the Lord protects in the midst of family dysfunction.

Don't focus on the imperfections of your family, but rather ask the Lord to work in the midst of what is happening and remember that your family member is a child of God just like you are!

Believe the Lord to do big things and if you don't have the faith for that, then ask the Lord to give you the faith that you need. He is consistent!

DAY 199

Genesis 28:20-22

20 Then Jacob made a vow, saying, "If God will be with me and will watch over me on this journey I am taking and will give me food to eat and clothes to wear 21 so that I return safely to my father's household, then the Lord will be my God 22 and this stone that I have set up as a pillar will be God's house, and of all that you give me I will give you a tenth."

This is a great reminder that we are called to give a tenth back to the Lord as He provides for us in this journey. We can follow Jacob's example, trusting that the Lord will provide and we can give back to Him. I am thankful for the example of the dependency Jacob had on the Lord.

What can we give back to the Lord today?

Day 200

Genesis 28:15-17

15 I am with you and will watch over you wherever you go, and I will bring you back to this land. I will not leave you until I have done what I have promised you.

16 When Jacob awoke from his sleep, he thought, "Surely the Lord is in this place, and I was not aware of it." 17 He was afraid and said, "How awesome is this place! This is none other than the house of God; this is the gate of heaven."

God said to Jacob, "I am with you and will watch over you wherever you go, and I will bring you back to this land. I will not leave you until I have done what I have promised you." (Verse 15)

This promise, alone, is such a peaceful reminder for me to hold on to no matter whether the road feels long and hopeless or I am content with what the Lord has set before me. The Lord promises us many things and He does not fail. His track record is spotless.

As I encounter different people in my job, I can see how the Lord would rather me focus on this promise of His that He will not leave me until he completes what He has promised. My mindset towards those who may be harder to work with or don't have a great track record in getting things done quickly changes when I choose to focus on the Lord.

Don't forget verses 16-17 too because they remind us to praise the Lord because HE IS IN THIS PLACE!

Day 201

Genesis 33:10

10 "No, please!" said Jacob. "If I have found favor in your eyes, accept this gift from me. For to see your face is like seeing the face of God, now that you have received me favorably."

Praise the Lord! It is always good to look back and remember where the Lord has brought you from. Back in 2013-2015, I went through a time when I was not serving in full-time ministry. It was a challenging season and the Lord taught me a lot about forgiveness and growing in love towards him, authority, and others around me. The Lord called me to persevere and trust Him for his timing.

He showed me Genesis 33:10 very early on, and encouraged me that returning to full-time ministry would be like seeing Him face to face; I would be received favorably by the ministry to which He was calling me to return. The Lord is so gracious!

Day 202

Genesis 42: 7-23

7 As soon as Joseph saw his brothers, he recognized them, but he pretended to be a stranger and spoke harshly to them. "Where do you come from?" he asked.

"From the land of Canaan," they replied, "to buy food."

8 Although Joseph recognized his brothers, they did not recognize him. 9 Then he remembered his dreams about them and said to them, "You are spies! You have come to see where our land is unprotected."

10 "No, my lord," they answered. "Your servants have come to buy food. 11 We are all the sons of one man. Your servants are honest men, not spies."

12 "No!" he said to them. "You have come to see where our land is unprotected."

13 But they replied, "Your servants were twelve brothers, the sons of one man, who live in the land of Canaan. The youngest is now with our father, and one is no more."

14 Joseph said to them, "It is just as I told you: You are spies! 15 And this is how you will be tested: As surely as Pharaoh lives, you will not

leave this place unless your youngest brother comes here. 16 Send one of your number to get your brother; the rest of you will be kept in prison, so that your words may be tested to see if you are telling the truth. If you are not, then as surely as Pharaoh lives, you are spies!" 17 And he put them all in custody for three days.

18 On the third day, Joseph said to them, "Do this and you will live, for I fear God: 19 If you are honest men, let one of your brothers stay here in prison, while the rest of you go and take grain back for your starving households. 20 But you must bring your youngest brother to me, so that your words may be verified and that you may not die." This they proceeded to do.

21 They said to one another, "Surely we are being punished because of our brother. We saw how distressed he was when he pleaded with us for his life, but we would not listen; that's why this distress has come on us."

22 Reuben replied, "Didn't I tell you not to sin against the boy? But you wouldn't listen! Now we must give an accounting for his blood." 23 They did not realize that Joseph could understand them, since he was using an interpreter.

Joseph didn't choose to see his brothers the way God sees them... children of God.

I have a particular individual in my life that I really struggle to see as a child of God. No, he isn't my sibling like Joseph dealt with. But, he is my brother in Christ. It is a slow learning process for me to not see this individual based on circumstances or his lack of follow through.

This passage of scripture is a good challenge to choose today to see this person as a child of God and ask God to help me see him as He wants me to see him.

I pray that each of us would take time to ask the Lord to help us see one another as children of God. He created us and loves us all the same. Let's walk in the light and trust God for how he wants to change our mindsets and our hearts toward others.

Day 203

Exodus 3:14

14 God said to Moses, "I am who I am.[a] This is what you are to say to the Israelites: 'I am has sent me to you.'"

Our God is the I AM. He is the same in Exodus as He is today. When everything else is crazy and you just want to pull your hair out — stop! Breathe! Remember the Lord is I AM! Allow that to quiet your heart and mind today.

Day 204

Exodus 18:14-27

14 When his father-in-law saw all that Moses was doing for the people, he said, "What is this you are doing for the people? Why do you alone sit as judge, while all these people stand around you from morning till evening?"

15 Moses answered him, "Because the people come to me to seek God's will. 16 Whenever they have a dispute, it is brought to me, and I decide between the parties and inform them of God's decrees and instructions." 17 Moses' father-in-law replied, "What you are doing is not good. 18 You and these people who come to you will only wear yourselves out. The work is too heavy for you; you cannot handle it alone. 19 Listen now to me and I will give you some advice, and may God be with you. You must be the people's representative before God and bring their disputes to him. 20 Teach them his decrees and instructions, and show them the way they are to live and how they are to behave. 21 But select capable men from all the people—men who fear God, trustworthy men who hate dishonest gain—and appoint them as officials over

thousands, hundreds, fifties and tens. 22 Have them serve as judges for the people at all times, but have them bring every difficult case to you; the simple cases they can decide themselves. That will make your load lighter, because they will share it with you. 23 If you do this and God so commands, you will be able to stand the strain, and all these people will go home satisfied."

24 Moses listened to his father-in-law and did everything he said. 25 He chose capable men from all Israel and made them leaders of the people, officials over thousands, hundreds, fifties and tens. 26 They served as judges for the people at all times. The difficult cases they brought to Moses, but the simple ones they decided themselves.

27 Then Moses sent his father-in-law on his way, and Jethro returned to his own country.

B urned out. Tired. Worn out. Alone. These are all words that described my life several years ago as I served in full-time ministry in my own strength. I was grateful to be placed in leadership roles, like Moses in this passage. But, I was running the show on my own because I knew my authority trusted me to get the job done. It is good to be confident in the gifts the Lord has given each one of us, but it is much more important to remember to "appoint others" just as Jethro told Moses to do. Otherwise we will get burned out and then we are not good to anyone.

If you are in a situation where you feel you can't ask for help or there seems to be no one available...that is just the enemy talking. No matter whether we are weak or strong, we can say with joy, "Not today Satan!" And then ask the Lord to show us who he would have us "appoint". Lean on the Lord and listen to his voice through those around you.

DAY 205

Exodus 31:18

18 When the Lord finished speaking to Moses
on Mount Sinai, he gave him the two tablets of
the covenant law, the tablets of stone inscribed
by the finger of God.

P ut yourself in Moses' shoes. First, you get to stand on Mount
Sinai before the Lord. Secondly, the Lord hands you two
tablets that he has inscribed with his own finger!

We could choose to read this verse and see it as a blah moment
in the Bible where God hands two stone tablets to Moses — with a
lot of rules. Ah yet it is so much more intimate than that. The close-
ness that Moses had with God. Beautiful. Sweet. Best gift ever!

DAY 206

Exodus 33:12-23

12 Moses said to the Lord, "You have been telling me, 'Lead these people,' but you have not let me know whom you will send with me. You have said, 'I know you by name and you have found favor with me.' 13 If you are pleased with me, teach me your ways so I may know you and continue to find favor with you. Remember that this nation is your people."

14 The Lord replied, "My Presence will go with you, and I will give you rest."

15 Then Moses said to him, "If your Presence does not go with us, do not send us up from here. 16 How will anyone know that you are pleased with me and with your people unless you go with us? What else will distinguish me and your people from all the other people on the face of the earth?"

17 And the Lord said to Moses, "I will do the very thing you have asked, because I am pleased with you and I know you by name."

18 Then Moses said, "Now show me your glory."

19 And the Lord said, "I will cause all my goodness to pass in front of you, and I will proclaim

my name, the Lord, in your presence. I will have mercy on whom I will have mercy, and I will have compassion on whom I will have compassion. 20 But," he said, "you cannot see my face, for no one may see me and live."

21 Then the Lord said, "There is a place near me where you may stand on a rock. 22 When my glory passes by, I will put you in a cleft in the rock and cover you with my hand until I have passed by. 23 Then I will remove my hand and you will see my back; but my face must not be seen."

Rest in this promise today, that the Lord's presence goes before you, He knows you by name and finds favor with you. I hope that you will just breathe the words of this passage.

Imagine how the God of the universe finds favor in YOU. How is this even possible that there is a God who loves ME and YOU so much that he finds favor in each of us? He knows us by name and His presence goes before us.

If that doesn't make you feel complete and at peace, what will?

Day 207

Exodus 33:11

11 The Lord would speak to Moses face to face,
as one speaks to a friend. Then Moses would
return to the camp, but his young aide Joshua
son of Nun did not leave the tent.

The once consistency in life, when all else is crazy or people
come and go from life, is God. he is our friend.

I have to admit, this verse is a little convicting for me, because
I fail to see God as a friend whom I can speak face to face with as
He did with Moses. Although it may be a conviction, it is also a
gracious reminder of who God is in our lives.

He is consistent and someone with whom we can speak face
to face. He is waiting with a listening ear and understanding heart!

Day 208

Exodus 34:10

10 Then the Lord said: "I am making a covenant with you. Before all your people I will do
wonders never before done in any nation in all
the world. The people you live among will see
how awesome is the work that I, the Lord, will
do for you.

This verse is so encouraging. As I read it, the GFA World US
office comes to mind. We are a small closely-knit community, but the Lord is doing incredible things through our ministry to impact many nations, as well as our local community of
Wills Point.

In a time of history where we have been pushed into times of
quarantining and isolation, it can be hard to see the impact of the
work the Lord is doing. But He is moving—just as he did among
the people of Moses' time.

Through GFA World's ministry in many Asian nations, we
have seen over 100,000 families helped through our COVID-19
relief efforts. Many are receiving bags of potatoes, vegetables, rice,
and other helpful items.

Today, I pray that we would each take a moment to look at
the needs of our local communities as well as internationally, to

see how the Lord wants to make an impact through the work He can do through us.

You can visit www.gfa.org/coronavirus <http://www.gfa.org/coronavirus> for just one of many ideas for getting involved to impact the world!

DAY 209

Exodus 34:5-7

5 Then the Lord came down in the cloud and stood there with him and proclaimed his name, the Lord. 6 And he passed in front of Moses, proclaiming, "The Lord, the Lord, the compassionate and gracious God, slow to anger, abounding in love and faithfulness, 7 maintaining love to thousands, and forgiving wickedness, rebellion and sin. Yet he does not leave the guilty unpunished; he punishes the children and their children for the sin of the parents to the third and fourth generation."

This is a great reminder that our God is a fair and just God! He will proclaim His name. He is compassionate, gracious, slow to anger. He is abounding in love and faithfulness.

Abounding! Read that word again. Abounding! Abounding in love and faithfulness.

The passage goes one to say that he is "maintaining love to thousands, and forgiving wickedness, rebellion, and sin."

That pretty much covers it!

I am sure you have caught on by now, but the recurring theme of this devotional is just to remember how good our God is. He is faithful and loving...and he forgives our sin! He is Everything Good and Beautiful!

DAY 210

Exodus 34:29-35

29 When Moses came down from Mount Sinai with the two tablets of the covenant law in his hands, he was not aware that his face was radiant because he had spoken with the Lord. 30 When Aaron and all the Israelites saw Moses, his face was radiant, and they were afraid to come near him. 31 But Moses called to them; so Aaron and all the leaders of the community came back to him, and he spoke to them. 32 Afterward all the Israelites came near him, and he gave them all the commands the Lord had given him on Mount Sinai.

33 When Moses finished speaking to them, he put a veil over his face. 34 But whenever he entered the Lord's presence to speak with him, he removed the veil until he came out. And when he came out and told the Israelites what he had been commanded, 35 they saw that his face was radiant. Then Moses would put the veil back over his face until he went in to speak with the Lord.

Reading this passage, my mind wanders to thoughts of my Granddad, Dane. He always had a twinkle in his eye, but even more so, he always had the radiance of the Lord on his face.

A radiance like I imagine Moses had after speaking to the Lord. Although my Granddad is no longer on this earth, it makes me smile with great joy to think of the radiance on his face as he gets to sit daily before the Lord in heaven.

In verse 29, "When Moses came down from Mount Sinai with the two tablets of the covenant law in his hands, he was not aware that his face was radiant because he had spoken with the Lord." Moses was unaware.

The following verses tell of how Moses called to Aaron and the leaders,. After speaking to them, he covered his face with a veil because it was so radiant. Today, I encourage you to spend time just thinking about what it would be like to experience the radiance of God in those around you! God truly loved Aaron and others so much that He allowed them to experience His radiance in Moses' face and then had Moses cover his face. They truly got the full package!

I am thankful for the many times I saw the radiance of God in my Granddad — it changes your whole relationship with a person.

I am overjoyed by the word "radiant"! A simple question for you today, what if you were to spend time with the Lord with the expectation that your face would be so radiant that you would have to cover your face?

As I write this particular devotional day, our world is now 9 months into the COVID-19 pandemic where we are having to wear masks when we go out in public. But reading this passage gives me a very different outlook on having to do life behind a mask. Maybe we spend time with the Lord and live today with faces that are covered because of the radiance of the Lord!!!

Day 211

Leviticus 19:18

18 "'Do not seek revenge or bear a grudge against anyone among your people, but love your neighbor as yourself. I am the Lord.

The command of, "Love your neighbor as yourself", is one that we hear in Sunday school a lot. But the way that verse 18 puts it gives a greater context. If you don't love yourself, how do you love your neighbor?

The context of the Lord telling us to not seek revenge or bear a grudge, is powerful. But, he doesn't just leave it at, "Love your neighbor as yourself".

No! He says, "Love your neighbor as yourself. I am the Lord." Because HE IS THE LORD, we get to choose to trust the Lord to show us how to love ourselves, and in turn, love our neighbors!

DAY 212

Leviticus 19:28
28 "'Do not cut your bodies for the dead or put tattoo marks on yourselves. I am the Lord.

There is definitely a verse in the bible for everything. Remember, the power of the statement, "I am the Lord."

Read Leviticus, otherwise you may miss out on a lot of good and beautiful things that the Lord wants to reveal to you.

DAY 213

Leviticus 19:32
32 "'Stand up in the presence of the aged, show respect for the elderly and revere your God. I am the Lord.

This is such a bold statement to me, especially in this day and age. The beauty of respecting our elders has become a thing of rarity. . Of course, it is always one of those "annoying" lessons you are told continuously as a kid, but now we know — it's biblical.

I can see that living out these three commands in this verse could present quite a challenge because in our American culture, we are not taught to stand up as a form of respect when an older person comes into the room. But in Asian cultures, it's a part of their daily life. Will you be brave and bold enough to go against the culture and live out this verse? How will that change your reverence towards the Lord?

Think about it.

Day 214

Leviticus 20:26

26 You are to be holy to me because I, the Lord, am holy, and I have set you apart from the nations to be my own.

There is so much peace and strength in this verse. No matter what you are facing today — good or bad — remember we are called to be holy because He is holy. He has set you apart to be His own!

Stand firm in this promise today.

DAY 215

Leviticus 25:17

17 Do not take advantage of each other, but fear
your God. I am the Lord your God.

I like how this verse is worded in the NLT version, "Show your
fear of God by not taking advantage of each other. I am the Lord
your God."

This is one of those verses that I would love to have written
on my hands as a good reminder! I don't say that because I live
my life taking advantage of others, but because it is just a good
reminder to live out — even when you feel you are being taken
advantage of. It is a good practice to look at those around you in
light of this verse.

Day 216

Leviticus 25:55

55 for the Israelites belong to me as servants. They are my servants, whom I brought out of Egypt. I am the Lord your God.

The proclamation of the Lord is incredible through this verse! He calls the Israelites His own — the ones he called out of Egypt. He reminds us of what He has done for the Israelites in just a few words and declares them as His servants!

We are continuously called to remember where we came from. What has the Lord done in your life today? This week? This month?

"They are my servants, whom I brought out of Egypt. I am the LORD your God." How can you personalize this sentence in this verse?

Mine might say something like, "Shareen is my servant for whom I have overcome migraines today. I am the LORD your God."

Wow! The power of His Word!!! Try it — you won't be disappointed!

DAY 217

Leviticus 26:40-42

40 "But if they will confess their sins and the sins of their ancestors—their unfaithfulness and their hostility toward me, 41 which made me hostile toward them so that I sent them into the land of their enemies—then when their uncircumcised hearts are humbled and they pay for their sin, 42 I will remember my covenant with Jacob and my covenant with Isaac and my covenant with Abraham, and I will remember the land.

God's wrath is for real. Yes, as we repent, he will take us back. He doesn't destroy the Israelites completely.

In this moment, if you find yourself carrying sins of which you have not repented before the Lord, take some time with HIm. He is waiting, full of love, grace, and the deepest of mercy for you, His child. Everything Good and Beautiful is waiting for you in His loving arms.

Day 218

Joshua 1:5-9

5 No one will be able to stand against you all the days of your life. As I was with Moses, so I will be with you; I will never leave you nor forsake you. 6 Be strong and courageous, because you will lead these people to inherit the land I swore to their ancestors to give them.

7 "Be strong and very courageous. Be careful to obey all the law my servant Moses gave you; do not turn from it to the right or to the left, that you may be successful wherever you go. 8 Keep this Book of the Law always on your lips; meditate on it day and night, so that you may be careful to do everything written in it. Then you will be prosperous and successful. 9 Have I not commanded you? Be strong and courageous. Do not be afraid; do not be discouraged, for the Lord your God will be with you wherever you go."

I have now written hundreds of devotionals and I am still finding myself completely baffled by passages like this one that declare we are to be strong and courageous. No matter how many times you read a passage such as this one, remember God's law. Keep it close and rely on its strength.

It's one thing to write that on a page, but what does it look like for you today, to hold to God's law and live courageously and strong?

I don't know about you, but it makes me feel powerful and like I can overcome ALL things through HIm— anger, sadness, frustrations, stress. You name it. Be strong and courageous. He's got you!

Day 219

Joshua 1:18

18 Whoever rebels against your word and does not obey it, whatever you may command them, will be put to death. Only be strong and courageous!"

"Only be strong and courageous." There will be people in our lives whom we will be asked to lead, whether that is your children, students in your classroom, a team of people at work — however we all are human and fall short. We can have seasons of disobedience and not want to listen. Through his promises though we have hope.

Start and end each day proclaiming God's promise to help you be strong and courageous. Try it. And see how today goes. There is a reason the Lord reminds Joshua so many times throughout chapter one of this simple, yet strengthening promise.

DAY 220

Joshua 3:17

17 The priests who carried the ark of the covenant of the Lord stopped in the middle of the Jordan and stood on dry ground, while all Israel passed by until the whole nation had completed the crossing on dry ground.

Reading verse 17 is just not enough. It is just the end of the story. If you have the time right now, I would encourage you to take time to read through chapter 3 — it is only 17 verses — yet, there is so much packed into this passage of God's awesomeness and power to lead his people.

Just a few questions to think through:

Are you willing to have a mindset of consecrating yourself, for tomorrow the Lord will do amazing things among you? (v. 5)

How is the Lord leading you through authorities in your life?

Pick a particular area in your life that is challenging. How do you see the Lord directing your steps in this area?

Now read verse 17 once more. If the WHOLE nation of Israel can cross the Jordan on dry land, just think of the awesome things the Lord will do for you today, tomorrow, and in the days to come!

Day 221

Hosea 6:6
6 For I desire mercy, not sacrifice,
and acknowledgment of God rather than burnt
offerings.

Today is a Monday for me, as I write this devotional. Monday where nothing seemed to be going right. I kept hitting roadblocks in my projects, and was growing very frustrated with life. Sometimes in the midst of anxiety or things not going right, it is hard to slow down and be quiet before the Lord. But, the Lord is patient and waiting.

On a day like today, where I just want to hit my deadlines and get things done… The Lord uses this verse as "the verse of the day". Sitting here now at the end of my day, the Lord quietly reminds me of this verse. There is no guilt or condemnation in his reminder, just peace and the beautiful realization that His desire is for me and for you to come sit at his feet and know Him.

We can be about the Lord's service and busy each day, but He desires a heart that knows him. I'm not one who sacrifices and brings spread offerings.

DAY 222

Joshua 4:20-24

20 And Joshua set up at Gilgal the twelve stones they had taken out of the Jordan. 21 He said to the Israelites, "In the future when your descendants ask their parents, 'What do these stones mean?' 22 tell them, 'Israel crossed the Jordan on dry ground.' 23 For the Lord your God dried up the Jordan before you until you had crossed over. The Lord your God did to the Jordan what he had done to the Red Sea[a] when he dried it up before us until we had crossed over. 24 He did this so that all the peoples of the earth might know that the hand of the Lord is powerful and so that you might always fear the Lord your God."

In a day and age where a pandemic is sweeping the world, we have seen many deaths of loved ones. This has me thinking, "What will people say about me at my memorial service?"

The stones of remembrance, representing a story of the past events, are a beautiful picture to show the glory of God. I don't know about you, but I want to leave a list of "stones of remembrance" behind when I leave this earth. Stones to represent that the power of the hand of the Lord is strong. May my life represent the fear of God — whether alive or in heaven. What will people see?

DAY 223

Joshua 10:42

42 All these kings and their lands Joshua conquered in one campaign, because the Lord, the
God of Israel, fought for Israel.

The word "campaign" in this verse strongly resonates with me.
The main focus of my administrative job is to create radio cam-
paigns that will help raise funds for needs throughout the countries in which GFA World serves.

Today, let's make this verse personal. "All these kings and their
lands [insert your name] conquered in one campaign, because
the LORD, the God of [insert your name], fought for [insert
your name]."

Maybe today, as you are reading this devotional, you have a
big project or a tough situation ahead of you. Remember, your
God is fighting for you and you will conquer the "kings and lands".
The thought of this verse and His power to fight for us, brings
me such joy.

We're going to make it, my friend!

DAY 224

Joshua 21:45

45 Not one of all the Lord's good promises to
Israel failed; every one was fulfilled.

Today is simple. Take time to hold on to His promises. Not
one of His good promises failed. Every one of His promises
will be fulfilled.

He's got this!

Day 225

Joshua 22:5

5 But be very careful to keep the commandment and the law that Moses the servant of the Lord gave you: to love the Lord your God, to walk in obedience to him, to keep his commands, to hold fast to him and to serve him with all your heart and with all your soul."

Five Things to Remember:

1. Love the Lord your God.

2. Walk in obedience to him.

3. Keep his commands.

4. Hold fast to him.

5. Serve him with all your heart and all your soul.

We can all create lists of tasks that we need to accomplish on a daily, weekly, monthly or annual basis. It's also easy to blow over a task you have seen a million times. The question, for me, becomes, "Am I actually used to that task because it is a normal practice in my daily life or do I just push it to the side?"

You don't have to consume this whole list above in one bite. Enjoy a small child-like bite and trust the Lord to grow you in that area for today or this week, or even the next month.

If we start small, we can conquer many things! Allow the Lord to fight for you.

DAY 226

Joshua 22:34

34 And the Reubenites and the Gadites gave the altar this name: A Witness Between Us—that the Lord is God.

This doesn't quite seem like a stand-alone verse. For the full context, go back and read all of chapter 22. As you read, look for points of hope and stability that explain why they came to a point of being able to call the altar, "A Witness Between Us— that the Lord is God."

B e faithful to the Lord.

DAY 227

Joshua 23:6

6 "Be very strong; be careful to obey all that is written in the Book of the Law of Moses, without turning aside to the right or to the left.

The Lord's commands are so simply said, but our flesh fights against them. Where do you need to take a moment and ask the Lord to refocus your mind so that you have the strength to look directly ahead in his word and obey his commands — not looking to the right or to the left?

Some days are harder and more distracting, yet the Lord encourages us to be careful to obey all that is written in the Book of the Law.

If you are reading today's devotional, hopefully that means that you have read the other 232 days and have read many commands and promises. Your mind should be full of beautiful verses that tell us to obey and trust the Lord. Don't look to the right or to the left. When your flesh cries out for you to look elsewhere, ask the Lord for the grace and strength to refocus. It's a good practice and it really works. Be patient.

Day 228

Joshua 23:8
8 But you are to hold fast to the Lord your God,
as you have until now.

Keep pressing into the Lord! Hold fast to the Lord your God as you've been doing. What glorious things is he speaking to you today? He wants you to hold fast in the midst of the rain clouds and the sunshine. It is so worth it. Just allow yourself to be awakened by your Heavenly Daddy!

DAY 229

Joshua 23:10
10 One of you routs a thousand, because the
Lord your God fights for you, just as he promised.

It is amazing how many times, throughout the book of Joshua, we read the phrase, "the Lord your God fights for you". We would benefit greatly to stand on that promise that our God fights for us. He didn't just do it once and move on. It's a recurring theme throughout his Word.

The life that comes from this simple promise is more than I can bear as it fills me with great joy to have my mind renewed in his word and know HE WILL FIGHT FOR ME because I am His and He (the God of the universe) is mine!!!

Day 230

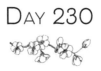

Joshua 23:11

11 So be very careful to love the Lord your God.

Be careful to love the Lord. These words are powerfully delicate. Be careful. To love. The Lord your God. This verse paints a picture of walking through a field with my God, hand in hand, telling him how much I love him as I look at the blades of grass and the blue skies. If it's a rainy day, I love him still through the clouds and the individual raindrops that he has created to water the ground and bring growth. Everything good and beautiful.

May the peace of God fill you today.

DAY 231

Joshua 23:14

14 "Now I am about to go the way of all the earth. You know with all your heart and soul that not one of all the good promises the Lord your God gave you has failed. Every promise has been fulfilled; not one has failed.

This verse is truly great. It starts with a sad view knowing death is coming. It speaks so boldly of the testimony of God's faithfulness in our lives. You know with all your heart and soul that not one of all the good promises the Lord your God gave you has failed.

Will the dash on your headstone represent this verse? If not, how does the LORD want to change you?

Day 232

Joshua 24:14-15

14 "Now fear the Lord and serve him with all faithfulness. Throw away the gods your ancestors worshiped beyond the Euphrates River and in Egypt, and serve the Lord. 15 But if serving the Lord seems undesirable to you, then choose for yourselves this day whom you will serve, whether the gods your ancestors served beyond the Euphrates, or the gods of the Amorites, in whose land you are living. But as for me and my household, we will serve the Lord."

"Now fear the Lord and serve him with all faithfulness."

The beauty of this passage is that we, as individuals, can go before the Lord and ask him specifically, "Lord, what does it mean to serve you with all faithfulness?"

The answer to this question may be similar, but different depending on each individual and where they are in life.

Verse 15 goes on to say, "But if serving the LORD seems undesirable to you..." — I find myself wanting to just chew on this part of the verse, not because serving the Lord is "undesirable" for me at this point in my life, but I know I have had those days where it is just difficult to serve the Lord or I just don't want to.

It doesn't end there! Joshua tells us what we are to do if we have this feeling of undesirability. He calls us to choose for ourselves who we will serve. This isn't a group decision. Just go to the LORD, one on one. Do what you want, but make a choice!

DAY 233

Joshua 24:23

23 "Now then," said Joshua, "throw away the foreign gods that are among you and yield your hearts to the Lord, the God of Israel."

There is so much thanksgiving and rest in the fact that God has created each of us intricately — different from one another. Each of us has hobbies and things we love or hate. We also have "foreign gods" that can consume our lives.

A challenge for today is to ask the Lord, "What are my foreign gods that keep me from yielding my heart to You?"

Honestly, you may not like the answer He gives you. Just be ready to be still and listen. He will show you the way.

Not one of his good promises fail.

DAY 234

Judges 3:20-25

20 Ehud then approached him while he was sitting alone in the upper room of his palace[a] and said, "I have a message from God for you." As the king rose from his seat, 21 Ehud reached with his left hand, drew the sword from his right thigh and plunged it into the king's belly. 22 Even the handle sank in after the blade, and his bowels discharged. Ehud did not pull the sword out, and the fat closed in over it. 23 Then Ehud went out to the porch[b]; he shut the doors of the upper room behind him and locked them.

24 After he had gone, the servants came and found the doors of the upper room locked. They said, "He must be relieving himself in the inner room of the palace." 25 They waited to the point of embarrassment, but when he did not open the doors of the room, they took a key and unlocked them. There they saw their lord fallen to the floor, dead.

Rejoice! Laugh! Allow the tears of laughter to fall from your eyes!! This is such an odd story! Today is simply a day to find humor in the Lord's handiwork. I love that God sees it fit to include this story in his Word!!

Day 235

Judges 6:6-16

6 Midian so impoverished the Israelites that they cried out to the Lord for help.

7 When the Israelites cried out to the Lord because of Midian, 8 he sent them a prophet, who said, "This is what the Lord, the God of Israel, says: I brought you up out of Egypt, out of the land of slavery. 9 I rescued you from the hand of the Egyptians. And I delivered you from the hand of all your oppressors; I drove them out before you and gave you their land. 10 I said to you, 'I am the Lord your God; do not worship the gods of the Amorites, in whose land you live.' But you have not listened to me."

11 The angel of the Lord came and sat down under the oak in Ophrah that belonged to Joash the Abiezrite, where his son Gideon was threshing wheat in a winepress to keep it from the Midianites. 12 When the angel of the Lord appeared to Gideon, he said, "The Lord is with you, mighty warrior."

13 "Pardon me, my lord," Gideon replied, "but if the Lord is with us, why has all this happened to us? Where are all his wonders that our ancestors

told us about when they said, 'Did not the Lord bring us up out of Egypt?' But now the Lord has abandoned us and given us into the hand of Midian."

14 The Lord turned to him and said, "Go in the strength you have and save Israel out of Midian's hand. Am I not sending you?"

15 "Pardon me, my lord," Gideon replied, "but how can I save Israel? My clan is the weakest in Manasseh, and I am the least in my family."

16 The Lord answered, "I will be with you, and you will strike down all the Midianites, leaving none alive."

D on't live in the "if's", live in the present where God is present with you. Personalize the presence of God.

DAY 236

Judges 6:35-40

35 He sent messengers throughout Manasseh, calling them to arms, and also into Asher, Zebulun and Naphtali, so that they too went up to meet them.

36 Gideon said to God, "If you will save Israel by my hand as you have promised— 37 look, I will place a wool fleece on the threshing floor. If there is dew only on the fleece and all the ground is dry, then I will know that you will save Israel by my hand, as you said." 38 And that is what happened. Gideon rose early the next day; he squeezed the fleece and wrung out the dew—a bowlful of water.

39 Then Gideon said to God, "Do not be angry with me. Let me make just one more request. Allow me one more test with the fleece, but this time make the fleece dry and let the ground be covered with dew." 40 That night God did so. Only the fleece was dry; all the ground was covered with dew.

Don't doubt His presence. If you do, know that he will show himself faithful no matter how many times you feel you need to test him.

DAY 237

Judges 7:1-15

1 Early in the morning, Jerub-Baal (that is, Gideon) and all his men camped at the spring of Harod. The camp of Midian was north of them in the valley near the hill of Moreh. 2 The Lord said to Gideon, "You have too many men. I cannot deliver Midian into their hands, or Israel would boast against me, 'My own strength has saved me.' 3 Now announce to the army, 'Anyone who trembles with fear may turn back and leave Mount Gilead.'" So twenty-two thousand men left, while ten thousand remained.

4 But the Lord said to Gideon, "There are still too many men. Take them down to the water, and I will thin them out for you there. If I say, 'This one shall go with you,' he shall go; but if I say, 'This one shall not go with you,' he shall not go." 5 So Gideon took the men down to the water. There the Lord told him, "Separate those who lap the water with their tongues as a dog laps from those who kneel down to drink." 6 Three hundred of them drank from cupped hands, lapping like dogs. All the rest got down on their knees to drink.

7 The Lord said to Gideon, "With the three hundred men that lapped I will save you and give the Midianites into your hands. Let all the others go home." 8 So Gideon sent the rest of the Israelites home but kept the three hundred, who took over the provisions and trumpets of the others.

Now the camp of Midian lay below him in the valley. 9 During that night the Lord said to Gideon, "Get up, go down against the camp, because I am going to give it into your hands. 10 If you are afraid to attack, go down to the camp with your servant Purah 11 and listen to what they are saying. Afterward, you will be encouraged to attack the camp." So he and Purah, his servant, went down to the outposts of the camp. 12 The Midianites, the Amalekites and all the other eastern peoples had settled in the valley, thick as locusts. Their camels could no more be counted than the sand on the seashore.

13 Gideon arrived just as a man was telling a friend his dream. "I had a dream," he was saying. "A round loaf of barley bread came tumbling into the Midianite camp. It struck the tent with such force that the tent overturned and collapsed." 14 His friend responded, "This can be nothing other than the sword of Gideon son of Joash, the Israelite. God has given the Midianites and the whole camp into his hands."

15 When Gideon heard the dream and its interpretation, he bowed down and worshiped. He
returned to the camp of Israel and called out,
"Get up! The Lord has given the Midianite camp
into your hands."

D o you ever look around and wonder why there never seems
to be enough people to get the work done that is overflowing
from your plate? Or maybe you are praying for more workers for
the harvest... but there is no answer from the Lord?

As a word of encouragement, I have been blessed to see
the Lord thinning out the "army" and I wonder, "What are you
doing, Lord?"

As you read this passage, you see how Gideon was obedient to
send away those who the Lord told him needed to go home. He
trusted the Lord and in the end, there was a great opportunity for
Gideon to praise the Lord for his provision.

As you wait for the Lord to provide whatever you are asking
him for, don't forget to praise Him and give testimony of all He is
doing! Allow your response to be to worship the Lord!

DAY 238

Judges 8:23
23 But Gideon told them, "I will not rule over you, nor will my son rule over you. The Lord will rule over you."

The Lord places people in our lives to lead us and guide us. It is good to trust the Lord in those individuals. Remember, though, that the Lord rules over you, not man.

Man will disappoint you as he is only human.

The Lord will rule over you.

DAY 239

James 2:13

13 because judgment without mercy will be shown to anyone who has not been merciful. Mercy triumphs over judgment.

It is June 30, 2021. As I was reading through James chapter 2 for my devotions this morning, I felt it pressed upon my heart that it would be good to pause the devotional entries on Judges and look at James 2:13 for today.

"Mercy triumphs over judgment." These four bold words hit me like a ton of bricks. Hearing and reading these words, so quickly silences the need to judge others or even to judge myself. I was speaking with someone just last night about how admitting I've hit my wall or have too much on my plate feels like defeat and failure.

The response I received was this, "Well, that's probably something to do with pride. So just repent and sleep. Christ isn't judging you, so you really don't have the liberty to do that. We are at our best in Christ when we are defeated in our own strength. Paul mentioned something about that. :)"

Accept Christ's mercy for you and for those around you today! Mercy triumphs over judgment! It's so beautiful!!!

Day 240

Judges 9;50-55

50 Next Abimelek went to Thebez and besieged
it and captured it. 51 Inside the city, however,
was a strong tower, to which all the men and
women—all the people of the city—had fled.
They had locked themselves in and climbed
up on the tower roof. 52 Abimelek went to the
tower and attacked it. But as he approached
the entrance to the tower to set it on fire, 53 a
woman dropped an upper millstone on his head
and cracked his skull.

54 Hurriedly he called to his armor-bearer,
"Draw your sword and kill me, so that they can't
say,'A woman killed him.'" So his servant ran him
through, and he died. 55 When the Israelites saw
that Abimelek was dead, they went home.

What an incredible story of death and pride and how it can
overtake one person in power to take the lives of many.
Yet, the simplicity of one woman on the roof — that's all it took.

With all the death and destruction that Abimelek created,
although it is awe full, what stands out to you in this story? For
me, it's the woman. I want to meet her and get her story. It is so

easy to focus on the negative and the bigger story, but what about that one woman who dropped something from the roof?

How are you making your story known? Or better yet, how are you making the story of someone across the world known?

Are we willing to proclaim the story of the one who is starving and had the opportunity to hear the love of Christ for the first time?

A woman cracked Abimelek's skull open, but Abimelek was prideful and didn't want people to know a woman was the cause of his death. Be the right voice today and speak the truth!

Day 241

Judges 10:1

10 After the time of Abimelek, a man of Issachar named Tola son of Puah, the son of Dodo, rose to save Israel. He lived in Shamir, in the hill country of Ephraim.

There is a person named Dodo. There is nothing deep and spiritual about today's devotional. No matter how your day started or how it will end, I encourage you to take a moment to laugh. Why? Because there is a person named Dodo in the Bible.

I am thinking outside of the box here and remembering the many times my siblings and I used the name "Dodo Bird" as a way of name calling. Clearly not the nicest thing to say, but thankfully we grow out of it. Laughter is healing.

DAY 242

Judges 11:24
24 Will you not take what your god Chemosh
gives you? Likewise, whatever the Lord our God
has given us, we will possess.

Today I challenge you to think through those things that the
Lord has given you. They may be things from the past that He
has done for you or future things he is asking you to trust him for.
Make a list. Ask the Lord how Hevwould like you to take posses-
sion of the things he is giving you. Just see what He says and trust
Him.. One step at a time.

Day 243

Judges 11:34-40

34 When Jephthah returned to his home in Mizpah, who should come out to meet him but his daughter, dancing to the sound of timbrels! She was an only child. Except for her he had neither son nor daughter. 35 When he saw her, he tore his clothes and cried, "Oh no, my daughter! You have brought me down and I am devastated. I have made a vow to the Lord that I cannot break."

36 "My father," she replied, "you have given your word to the Lord. Do to me just as you promised, now that the Lord has avenged you of your enemies, the Ammonites. 37 But grant me this one request," she said. "Give me two months to roam the hills and weep with my friends, because I will never marry."

38 "You may go," he said. And he let her go for two months. She and her friends went into the hills and wept because she would never marry. 39 After the two months, she returned to her father, and he did to her as he had vowed. And she was a virgin.

From this comes the Israelite tradition 40 that each year the young women of Israel go out for four days to commemorate the daughter of Jephthah the Gileadite.

For the dads of daughters, how are you keeping your promises to the Lord regarding your daughter(s)? This may be a simple question to answer. But maybe it isn't. Do you know what promises the Lord has given you?

As a daughter, I can ask myself the same kind of questions. No, the Lord has never put my dad and me in a situation where it meant he had to be faithful to the Lord even to the point of sacrificing me. Yet, as I get older and am still single, the Lord has given me a different view of my dad than I had when I was a teen. I have a greater appreciation for him and want to learn from him as I face life's different situations.

How are you being faithful to the Lord — even to the point of sacrifice?

Day 244

Judges 14:16
16 Then Samson's wife threw herself on him, sobbing, "You hate me! You don't really love me. You've given my people a riddle, but you haven't told me the answer."

" haven't even explained it to my father or mother," he replied, "so why should I explain it to you?"

There is truly something in the Bible for every situation. Funny how even way back then, women used the line, "You hate me. You don't love me."

Chapter 14 is an incredible story worth reading to the end.

DAY 245

Judges 16:15

15 Then she said to him, "How can you say, 'I love you,' when you won't confide in me? This is the third time you have made a fool of me and haven't told me the secret of your great strength."

This is such an interesting verse which could very easily be taken out of context if it is read by itself.

"How can you say, 'I love you,' when you won't confide in me?"

This is a story of a woman who nagged her husband to tell her the secret of his strength and then used it against him. This verse alone brings a desperate cry for help as though she is the innocent one who is being treated unfairly by her husband.

No matter what your story may be today, remember there are always two sides to every story. As hard as it may be, take a moment to ask the Lord to:

Change your heart that your thoughts about other persons in your story may be honoring towards Him.

Open your eyes and heart to see what He wants to reveal to you.

Be willing to trust the Lord for whatever He reveals — good or bad, beautiful or ugly — He is ready to walk you through it and trust you with the trial(s).

Day 246

Judges 16:19–22

19 After putting him to sleep on her lap, she called for someone to shave off the seven braids of his hair, and so began to subdue him.[a] And his strength left him.

20 Then she called, "Samson, the Philistines are upon you!"

He awoke from his sleep and thought, "I'll go out as before and shake myself free." But he did not know that the Lord had left him.

21 Then the Philistines seized him, gouged out his eyes and took him down to Gaza. Binding him with bronze shackles, they set him to grinding grain in the prison. 22 But the hair on his head began to grow again after it had been shaved.

This story is so twisted, but it shows the power of the imperfections of humans and the strength of God. Samson's head was shaved and his strength left him. The Philistines gouged out his eyes.

Have there been times in your life that it is clear that the Lord (your strength) has left you? It isn't easy and, honestly, Samson's story is a rather heavy one.

Hold on tight. When we are weak and lonely, just wait.

Day 247

Judges 16:25-30

25 While they were in high spirits, they shouted, "Bring out Samson to entertain us." So they called Samson out of the prison, and he performed for them.

When they stood him among the pillars, 26 Samson said to the servant who held his hand, "Put me where I can feel the pillars that support the temple, so that I may lean against them." 27 Now the temple was crowded with men and women; all the rulers of the Philistines were there, and on the roof were about three thousand men and women watching Samson perform. 28 Then Samson prayed to the Lord, "Sovereign Lord, remember me. Please, God, strengthen me just once more, and let me with one blow get revenge on the Philistines for my two eyes." 29 Then Samson reached toward the two central pillars on which the temple stood. Bracing himself against them, his right hand on the one and his left hand on the other, 30 Samson said, "Let me die with the Philistines!" Then he pushed with all his might, and down came the temple on the rulers and all the people in it. Thus he killed many more when he died than while he lived.

This story is so sick and twisted. It is filled with the glorification of a false god who supposedly delivered Samson into the Philistine's hands, and about finding entertainment in showing cruelty to others. I realize this portion is not the most pleasant way to focus your mind in God's word, but I am so glad that Samson's story is in the Bible.

If we didn't have stories like this, we wouldn't have the strengthening reminder of how good our God has been in hearing our prayers as we cry out for the things that break his heart. There are incredibly devastating things going on throughout Asian countries, in our current day and age. Stories of people hiding in fear from those who want to harm them and many lives lost because of an increase in persecution.

What our world is facing today is unfathomable and hard to wrap our minds around. But God! If you look at verse 28, it says, "Then Samson prayed to the LORD, 'Sovereign LORD, remember me. Please, God, strengthen me just once more, and let me with one blow get revenge on the Philistines for my two eyes." Whether it be for yourself, a friend, a family member, or a soul on the other side of the world whom you don't even know — may our prayer for today be, "Sovereign LORD, remember me. Please, God, strengthen me just once more…"

There is a reason "LORD" is fully capitalized. Think about it. Pray. Lean into Him for His strength. Then let the pillars fall.

DAY 248

2 Samuel 4:9-11

9 David answered Rekab and his brother Baanah, the sons of Rimmon the Beerothite, "As surely as the Lord lives, who has delivered me out of every trouble, 10 when someone told me, 'Saul is dead,' and thought he was bringing good news, I seized him and put him to death in Ziklag. That was the reward I gave him for his news! 11 How much more—when wicked men have killed an innocent man in his own house and on his own bed—should I not now demand his blood from your hand and rid the earth of you!"

Have you ever noticed how hard it can be to speak truth to someone? That truthful word isn't always a field full of daisies and joy. This passage is one of those "hard truth" passages. There is a reason the Lord had Dave speak such words. Evil men should not kill the innocent, for they too will be put to death.

The application is obvious: Evil men should not kill the innocent. As you think about the evil in this world, would you take some time and pray for the "evil" men? The Lord has power to change the hearts of man, so we trust him for that change. Let us go to battle on our knees for those who need to be changed by His love. May the Spirit intercede and show himself true on behalf of your prayers today.

Day 249

2 Samuel 6:21-22

21 David said to Michal, "It was before the Lord, who chose me rather than your father or anyone from his house when he appointed me ruler over the Lord's people Israel—I will celebrate before the Lord. 22 I will become even more undignified than this, and I will be humiliated in my own eyes. But by these slave girls you spoke of, I will be held in honor."

The last few days of this devotional have contained heavy situations to think through. I don't know about you, but I am feeling a little bit weighed down. Although we saw the glory of the LORD through his word, it's been heavy.

The Lord is continually doing so much in our lives and the lives of others. He is growing His Kingdom and, I trust, that He is growing you in having more of a Kingdom-centered mindset. Today is a day to just close your eyes and allow yourself to be undignified as you rejoice in the Lord as David did. Let go. He is doing a new thing!

DAY 250

2 Samuel 8:6 & 14

6 He put garrisons in the Aramean kingdom of Damascus, and the Arameans became subject to him and brought tribute. The Lord gave David victory wherever he went.

14 He put garrisons throughout Edom, and all the Edomites became subject to David. The Lord gave David victory wherever he went.

Reading the phrase, "The LORD gave David victory wherever he went", brings so much freedom and joy to my mind. I dare you to think outside of the box today and put your name in place of David's name in this phrase.

"The LORD gave [your name] victory wherever [he/she] went."

No matter what point of your day you are reading this, write down how the LORD has done this in your day OR how you would like to see Him do this in the coming hours. At the end of the day, go back and see how He moved!

DAY 251

2 Samuel 22:2-4

2 He said: "The Lord is my rock, my fortress and
my deliverer;
3 my God is my rock, in whom I take refuge,
my shield[a] and the horn[b] of my salvation.
He is my stronghold, my refuge and my savior—
from violent people you save me.
4 "I called to the Lord, who is worthy of praise,
and have been saved from my enemies.

Stop. Slow down. Quiet your heart to see deep into these verses.
The Lord is my Rock.

The Lord is my fortress.

The Lord is my deliverer.

What does it mean to you to have the Lord be these three
different things to you? Maybe you are at a place where you need
to take one minute at a time or one hour at a time to ask yourself
such a question. Use this as a way to center your mind on the Lord
throughout today. He never gives you more than you can handle.

Day 252

2 Samuel 22:17-20

17 "He reached down from on high and took hold of me; he drew me out of deep waters.

18 He rescued me from my powerful enemy, from my foes, who were too strong for me.

19 They confronted me in the day of my disaster, but the Lord was my support.

20 He brought me out into a spacious place; he rescued me because he delighted in me.

Do you ever feel like you are in over your head? Or maybe you just want to be plunged into deep waters to feel a sense of refreshment? The Lord is ready to bring you out of deep waters and to deliver you. Even more so, He delights in you and wants to do this for you!

Now, I understand, you may be in a really dark place today as you read this and your flesh may be screaming at you to not believe the mighty truth spoken in these verses. But my friend, I am here to tell you — it is worth it! Your Daddy deeply delights in you and will deliver you from the deep waters!

Day 253

2 Samuel 22:26-27

26 "To the faithful you show yourself faithful, to the blameless you show yourself blameless,

27 to the pure you show yourself pure, but to the devious you show yourself shrewd.

To the faithful, You are faithful. Blameless to the blameless. Remember who He is to you today and think on these things.

Day 254

2 Samuel 22:32-36

32 For who is God besides the Lord?
And who is the Rock except our God?
33 It is God who arms me with strength[a]
and keeps my way secure.
34 He makes my feet like the feet of a deer;
he causes me to stand on the heights.
35 He trains my hands for battle;
my arms can bend a bow of bronze.
36 You make your saving help my shield;
your help has made[b] me great.

Take a moment to look at your hands. Have you ever thought that God has trained them for battle? May you take the challenge today to seize the moment and face today knowing God has trained your hands. He has given you a shield and will guide you in his way!

DAY 255

1 Kings 2:2-3

2 "I am about to go the way of all the earth," he said. "So be strong, act like a man, 3 and observe what the Lord your God requires: Walk in obedience to him, and keep his decrees and commands, his laws and regulations, as written in the Law of Moses. Do this so that you may prosper in all you do and wherever you go

As a believer in Christ, it is so easy to put on a happy face and pretend that life is good. Right? Isn't that what we do? We quote scripture and sing songs of worship, but do we actually live our lives believing that it is worth it to walk in obedience and follow His commands?

Read the above verses again. Stop. Think about it. Ask yourself at this moment, is it worth it to walk in obedience to the Lord and follow what he has said?

If your answer is "no", I am here to tell you that answer is OK. It is okay to not be okay. But don't stay there. I write this particular devotional in a time in my life where God was actively moving and I stepped out in faith in a really big way as the Lord led. The thing is, my friend, the door didn't open quite like I thought it would. Is it worth walking in obedience to the Lord?

Be faithful in the dry times. Be consistent in following his commands. Why? The answer at the end of verse 3 says, "...Do this so that you may prosper in all you do and whoever you go."

Day 256

1 Chronicles 5:20
20 They were helped in fighting them, and God delivered the Hagrites and all their allies into their hands, because they cried out to him during the battle. He answered their prayers, because they trusted in him.

The silence seems deafening and there isn't a direct word from the Lord. I certainly will be the first person to say that this verse is a nice verse of, "Yes! Pray in the battle. Trust the Lord. He will answer!" What happens when you are in the midst of a very "silence-filled" battle? Right? It's not easy. Yet, a verse like this one is so loud and blaring. It is filled with words of a reminder that we must stand our ground against an enemy who wants to harden our hearts and minds when we don't see the Lord answer a prayer in a way that we thought he was going to.

I speak from experience, though, that as I have stayed consistent in his Word, it makes it easier to hold on tight to his promises.

Ask the Lord to help you be OK with the silence. He hasn't left you. He hasn't left me.

Day 257

1 Chronicles 17:25
25 "You, my God, have revealed to your servant
that you will build a house for him. So your servant has found courage to pray to you.

This verse is a great promise of how God reveals and gives us
courage to seek Him. In this season of waiting upon the Lord,
I sense that the Lord is using this verse to show me how he has
revealed and established that he will answer my prayers for the
desires he has given me. With the things he has already revealed
over the last several months, I have the courage to pray to Him!
Praise the Lord!

Day 258

Ezra 3:3

3 Despite their fear of the peoples around them, they built the altar on its foundation and sacrificed burnt offerings on it to the Lord, both the morning and evening sacrifices.

Today's world is crazy and it is only getting crazier for the Church. As believers, I pray that we will not stay in our little bubble of quietly living for the Lord, but that we would make a difference — despite any fear of those around us.

DAY 259

Ezra 7:10

10 For Ezra had devoted himself to the study and observance of the Law of the Lord, and to teaching its decrees and laws in Israel.

Today is simple. Find ways to devote yourself to the Lord and his Word. Speak what He shows you through his Word. Create an impact and let Him shine through you.

Day 260

Revelation 12:4-11, 14

4 Its tail swept a third of the stars out of the sky and flung them to the earth. The dragon stood in front of the woman who was about to give birth, so that it might devour her child the moment he was born. 5 She gave birth to a son, a male child, who "will rule all the nations with an iron scepter." And her child was snatched up to God and to his throne. 6 The woman fled into the wilderness to a place prepared for her by God, where she might be taken care of for 1,260 days.

7 Then war broke out in heaven. Michael and his angels fought against the dragon, and the dragon and his angels fought back. 8 But he was not strong enough, and they lost their place in heaven. 9 The great dragon was hurled down— that ancient serpent called the devil, or Satan, who leads the whole world astray. He was hurled to the earth, and his angels with him.

10 Then I heard a loud voice in heaven say:
"Now have come the salvation and the powe
and the kingdom of our God
and the authority of his Messiah.
For the accuser of our brothers and sisters,

who accuses them before our God day and night,
has been hurled down.
11 They triumphed over him
by the blood of the Lamb
and by the word of their testimony;
they did not love their lives so much
as to shrink from death.
14 The woman was given the two wings of a great
eagle, so that she might fly to the place prepared
for her in the wilderness, where she would be
taken care of for a time, times and half a time,
out of the serpent's reach.

R evelation chapter 12 is filled with strong imagery of the
woman God protected and provided for, as well as that of
the dragon who is out to get her and her offspring. It is quite the
adventurous chapter to read. A little dark at times, but the Lord's
covering shows through very boldly!

As you read through this chapter, God's interaction with the
woman is that of protecting her from the dragon, which we later
find out is the devil. As God sends her to the earth after she gives
birth, he gives her a place to be cared for. When the devil becomes
angry because his strength is not enough to win the war, God gives
the woman two eagle's wings to fly to a place of protection. Over
and over, the Lord protects the woman.

In the beginning in the Garden of Eden, the devil plays a sig-
nificant part in interacting with a woman — Eve. Although God
was very clear in his instruction to Adam and Eve about which tree

not to eat from, the devil comes along and talks Eve into eating from it. As they ate, Adam and Eve were then found naked and felt the need to hide from God.

God had a plan of protection, but Eve chose a different route. It is interesting to me how Eve and the woman in Revelation had the same God — who never changes from day to day — desiring to protect, yet their outcomes were very different. They were both hidden, but Eve was hiding out of shame and the woman from Revelation fell into God's protective ways and was given eagle's wings to fly and be protected from the devil.

The devil knows his time is short. He will try all his tactics to tempt and destroy you minute by minute. But, God is waiting and ready to protect — to give you eagle's wings to fly. Be open to those wings! I guarantee you won't be disappointed!

Day 261

Ezra 10:9-11

9 Within the three days, all the men of Judah and Benjamin had gathered in Jerusalem. And on the twentieth day of the ninth month, all the people were sitting in the square before the house of God, greatly distressed by the occasion and because of the rain. 10 Then Ezra the priest stood up and said to them, "You have been unfaithful; you have married foreign women, adding to Israel's guilt. 11 Now honor[a] the Lord, the God of your ancestors, and do his will. Separate yourselves from the peoples around you and from your foreign wives."

What are you doing today? Are you sitting around before the house of the Lord feeling distressed? To that I would say, "Now honor the Lord, the God of your ancestors, and do his will."

We often can sit around and feel sorry for ourselves because things didn't go our way. If I am honest with myself, I have struggled with feeling sorry for myself because I took every step the Lord gave me and the outcome wasn't how I thought it was going to end up. Just because something doesn't go as we think, doesn't mean we should stop being faithful to the Lord and do our own thing.

In this stage of life I am in, the Lord continually reminds me that I did what he asked me to do. He directed me and I followed him by faith. No matter what doubt comes my way, I can say, "Now honor the Lord...and do his will." (Even if I have to repeat it a million times a day...I can choose to feel bad about the situation or I can honor the Lord and stay faithful!)

Day 262

Job 1:1, 8-10

1 In the land of Uz there lived a man whose name was Job. This man was blameless and upright; he feared God and shunned evil.

8 Then the Lord said to Satan, "Have you considered my servant Job? There is no one on earth like him; he is blameless and upright, a man who fears God and shuns evil."

9 "Does Job fear God for nothing?" Satan replied.

10 "Have you not put a hedge around him and his household and everything he has? You have blessed the work of his hands, so that his flocks and herds are spread throughout the land.

As we jump into the book of Job, it has a strong opening in describing who Job is and the legacy he has left! He is a man who is blameless and upright. He feared God and shunned evil.

Satan came along with the angels as they came to present themselves to the Lord. The Lord directs his attention to Satan and asks, "Have you considered my servant Job?" Job is like no one else on the earth. The Lord speaks so highly of Job.

How does the Lord think of you? He is never disappointed in us. He loves and forgives. He redeems. He challenges us to be remain faithful to him.

Will you do that today, no matter the temptation of Satan?

Oh that we would be blameless before the Lord and fear him on this earth!

DAY 263

Job 1:20-22

20 At this, Job got up and tore his robe and
shaved his head. Then he fell to the ground in
worship 21 and said:

"Naked I came from my mother's womb,
 and naked I will depart.[a]
The Lord gave and the Lord has taken away;
 may the name of the Lord be praised."

22 In all this, Job did not sin by charging God
with wrongdoing.

"The Lord gave and the Lord has taken away. May
 the name of the Lord be praised."

We have seen a lot of unimaginable loss in our world in the
midst of the Covid pandemic. Much of the loss has not
had closure for loved ones left on this earth because we couldn't
gather in person.

Looking at this passage, I am amazed at Job's response. It
seems so heartless. He has his kids taken from him by death and
many others who he loved. There is a reason the Lord placed passages such as this one in His Word and, truly, I am thankful that
He did. It creates a safe place to wrestle with grief and loss as there
are many emotions that come with grief.

When my Granddad passed away several years ago, he was the first person that I lost with whom I was very close. In that loss, there was joy because my family knew he was in heaven standing before the Lord, getting to meet with all those who had gone before him.

But I also remember coming home and the innumerable tears that fell from my eyes for several days as I processed and grieved. Going through that process gave me a new appreciation for those who grieve whether it is due to the death of a loved one or a friend who moves away. Grief is real and hard. And it is a process to get to the place where Job was and to respond as he did.

If you are in a place of grief or know someone who is, sometimes saying nothing is the best thing you can do. I pray that you will be open to wrestle with the Lord and allow him to take you through the full grief process to the other side. Be patient. He can handle it!

Day 264

Job 2:10

10 He replied, "You are talking like a foolish[a] woman. Shall we accept good from God, and not trouble?"

Question: Should we accept good from God and not trouble? In my sarcasm, I would respond, "Of course we should ONLY receive good from the Lord!" But then I fall silent because there is so much power in receiving "trouble" from the Lord.

Think about it. If we only get good things from the Lord and life is happy all the time, what is the point of living? How would we get to see God's goodness, mercy, and faithfulness in the midst of trouble? I am stronger for the trouble. I don't always like the trials and the trouble, nor the challenges.

Yet I wouldn't trade those hard times for anything.

If you are reading this and think I am just another positive Christian devotional writer to make you feel good for the day, I am not. I am legally blind and life has many challenges and dark places for me. Be encouraged. I speak out of my dark places more than anywhere else. Everything good and beautiful.

DAY 265

Job 3:1-10

1 After this, Job opened his mouth and cursed the day of his birth. 2 He said:

3 "May the day of my birth perish,

and the night that said, 'A boy is conceived!'

4 That day—may it turn to darkness;

may God above not care about it;

may no light shine on it.

5 May gloom and utter darkness claim it once more;

may a cloud settle over it;

may blackness overwhelm it.

6 That night—may thick darkness seize it;

may it not be included among the days of the year

nor be entered in any of the months.

7 May that night be barren;

may no shout of joy be heard in it.

8 May those who curse days[a] curse that day,

those who are ready to rouse Leviathan.

9 May its morning stars become dark;

may it wait for daylight in vain

and not see the first rays of dawn,

10 for it did not shut the doors of the womb on me

to hide trouble from my eyes.

The Bible holds truth for the darkest of dark places we can go in life. Not everyone has had an experience like Job where they want to curse the day they were born, but that doesn't mean that it doesn't happen. The heaviness in my heart after reading these verses is overwhelming. It reminds me, though, that the Lord wants to meet us right where we are.

Verses like these show me that it is totally okay to give the Lord all my emotions, my ups, my downs, my dark places and my places of deep joy in Him. He will stand by me in all things and in all places.

He will do the same for you — draw near to him!

Day 266

Job 4:2-6

2 "If someone ventures a word with you, will you
be impatient?
But who can keep from speaking?
3 Think how you have instructed many,
how you have strengthened feeble hands.
4 Your words have supported those who stumbled;
you have strengthened faltering knees.
5 But now trouble comes to you, and you are
discouraged;
it strikes you, and you are dismayed.
6 Should not your piety be your confidence
and your blameless ways, your hope?

Think of how you have encouraged and helped so many by your words. Shouldn't the fact that you have blameless ways be your hope?

Day 267

Job 5:1, 8-13, 17-18

"Call if you will, but who will answer you?
To which of the holy ones will you turn?
⁸ "But if I were you, I would appeal to God;
I would lay my cause before him.
⁹ He performs wonders that cannot be fathomed,
miracles that cannot be counted.
¹⁰ He provides rain for the earth;
he sends water on the countryside.
¹¹ The lowly he sets on high,
and those who mourn are lifted to safety.
¹² He thwarts the plans of the crafty,
so that their hands achieve no success.
¹³ He catches the wise in their craftiness,
and the schemes of the wily are swept away.
¹⁷ "Blessed is the one whom God corrects;
so do not despise the discipline of the Almighty.[a]
¹⁸ For he wounds, but he also binds up;
he injures, but his hands also heal.

Wow! I really like Job's friend Eliphaz because he is very blunt, yet continually points you back to the Lord and the hope the Lord gives as He calls us to be blameless and upright.

Chapter 5 is just totally jam-packed with so many great truths to hold onto no matter what you are facing, because it has great reminders of how faithful God truly is. Praise the Lord! I love it. Eliphaz is like, "Dude! Who are you going to call out to if you are cursing the day you were born or even the fact you were put on this earth? If I were you, I would present your request to God, because he does wonders that cannot be fathomed and miracles that cannot be counted."

Eliphaz goes on to say, in verses 12-13, how God thwarts the plans of the wicked (crafty), so that they have no success. God does all these great and mighty things, the one He corrects is blessed. So, don't despise the discipline of the Almighty! No matter how painful a season may be, God's got your back! His Word speaks of how He thwarts the plans of the crafty, so they have no success. In the end of all this You will grow strong and mighty! You will be so much more blessed, because through this discipline, He is refining you to make you more like Him!

Take a moment to thank the Lord for good friends who will speak truth into your life and point you back to Jesus!

DAY 268

Job 7:17-21

17 "What is mankind that you make so
much of them,
that you give them so much attention,
18 that you examine them every morning
and test them every moment?
19 Will you never look away from me,
or let me alone even for an instant?
20 If I have sinned, what have I done to you,
you who see everything we do?
Why have you made me your target?
Have I become a burden to you?[a]
21 Why do you not pardon my offenses
and forgive my sins?
For I will soon lie down in the dust;
you will search for me, but I will be no more."

I recently wrote a letter to someone because I strongly sensed the Lord leading me to write it. I knew it had to be from the Lord because I really struggled to stick it in the mailbox and let go of it in order to trust the Lord with the outcome. As I have referenced over the last few days, the outcome was very different than what I expected it would be. I was shocked and, in one sense or another, I had to talk through the stages of grief.

It was a huge step of faith to send the letter and I thought the Lord was crazy for asking me to do it, but I stepped out. I walked faithfully before the Lord.

But there was only disappointment in the end. I put on a happy face to hide my numbing pain. Little did I know that this passage of scripture was on the docket for me to write about in my devotional. The words of Job to the Lord bring a sense of safety in asking the "Why?"

In your personal time with the Lord, don't be afraid to ask the Lord "Why?" When you don't understand why a situation played out as it did, don't just chalk it up to, "Well, that's just the Lord's will." Maybe it is the Lord's will, but don't despise the discipline and the beauty that he wants to continue to bring out of a situation. Keep knocking. Keep seeking. Keep asking. You won't be disappointed and neither will He.

DAY 269

Job 8:13-15

13 Such is the destiny of all who forget God;
so perishes the hope of the godless.
14 What they trust in is fragile[a];
what they rely on is a spider's web.
15 They lean on the web, but it gives way;
they cling to it, but it does not hold.

For those of you who hate spiders, the moral of this passage today is: Those who forget God are like one who leans on a spider web, but it gives way.

Don't forget God.

Day 270

Job 8:5-6
5 But if you will seek God earnestly
and plead with the Almighty,
6 if you are pure and upright,
even now he will rouse himself on your behalf
and restore you to your prosperous state.

Have you ever had those days where you just didn't have the energy to seek the Lord earnestly about something? You know you should pray about a situation, but you aren't quite sure where to start! Lately, my mind has felt a little blank on the "future planning" front, as though there are too many options to even know where to begin to seek the Lord's direction.

How does the process begin? How do we seek the Lord earnestly when the buffet of options is too large? Start small. It doesn't have to be a big production of laying every bit of the plan out before the Lord. Be earnest in seeking Him. Be pure and upright. His Word says that He will arouse himself on your behalf and restore you. Rest in that promise!

Day 271

Job 8:19-21

19 Surely its life withers away,

and[a] from the soil other plants grow.

20 "Surely God does not reject one who is blameless

or strengthen the hands of evildoers.

21 He will yet fill your mouth with laughter

and your lips with shouts of joy.

B e blameless. He will fill your mouth with laughter and your lips with shouts of joy!

Day 272

Job 11:1-6

1 Then Zophar the Naamathite replied:
2 "Are all these words to go unanswered?
Is this talker to be vindicated?
3 Will your idle talk reduce others to silence?
Will no one rebuke you when you mock?
4 You say to God, 'My beliefs are flawless
and I am pure in your sight.'
5 Oh, how I wish that God would speak,
that he would open his lips against you
6 and disclose to you the secrets of wisdom,
for true wisdom has two sides.
Know this: God has even forgotten some
of your sin.

There was a very close friend in my life who had gone through a time where she really questioned God and didn't believe in him. She would continuously tell me of her unbelief, which would only push me more into His word to disprove her. Her talk was idle and frustrating. I wanted God to show her his wisdom and restore her to faith — but that wasn't up to me.

If you are in a situation with someone who is struggling to see the truth, be reminded that there are two sides to true wisdom.

DAY 273

Job 11:13-16

13 "Yet if you devote your heart to him
and stretch out your hands to him,
14 if you put away the sin that is in your hand
and allow no evil to dwell in your tent,
15 then, free of fault, you will lift up your face;
you will stand firm and without fear.
16 You will surely forget your trouble,
recalling it only as waters gone by.

What an incredible promise! Do you see how many times Job's friends point him back to God? Devote yourself to God.

Today, stretch out your hand to God, be open-handed with your sin and you will stand firm without fear. Do you believe that today? I pray that these verses will wash over you and that you will find a deepening strength from your Heavenly Daddy!

There is greater power in the words of scripture than in my own words.

Just read these 4 verses again and again.

DAY 274

Job 19:4

4 If it is true that I have gone astray,
my error remains my concern alone.

My personality is such that I desire to gain wisdom and insight from those in authority or those I trust, rather than running directly to the Lord. It is good to have people in our lives that will push us to the Lord, but don't forget the importance of keeping things just between you and the Lord. It's okay to keep your personal life personal.

DAY 275

Job 19:25-27

25 I know that my Redeemer[a] lives,

and that in the end he will stand on the earth.[b]

26 And after my skin has been destroyed,

yet[c] in[d] my flesh I will see God;

27 I myself will see him

with my own eyes—I, and not another.

How my heart yearns within me!

We can learn so much from Job. He is one who was called blameless before God, lost everything, and put through the wringer. In our human understanding, there is no reason why this man should go on with life or have hope for the future.

Verses 25-27 speak differently with a boldness of holding on to the One who is to come. The One he calls his Redeemer. I know my Redeemer lives and that in the end, I will see Him! I will see Him, not another. But, oh, how we should long for that day!

Keep hoping. He will make everything good and beautiful.

DAY 276

Job 22:1-3

1 Then Eliphaz the Temanite replied:

2 Can a man be of benefit to God?

Can even a wise person benefit him?

3 What pleasure would it give the Almighty if you were righteous?

What would he gain if your ways were blameless?

What pleasure would God get if we were righteous or blameless? We would truly have no need for God. That is a bit of a terrifying thought to have no need for God. May we today come before our Heavenly Daddy and just thank him that we GET to be dependent on him. Even when things aren't going right, our God is still there and ready to listen. He is our helper in times of need.

DAY 277

Job 22:21-30

21 "Submit to God and be at peace with him;
in this way prosperity will come to you.
22 Accept instruction from his mouth
and lay up his words in your heart.
23 If you return to the Almighty, you will
be restored:
If you remove wickedness far from your tent
24 and assign your nuggets to the dust,
your gold of Ophir to the rocks in the ravines,
25 then the Almighty will be your gold,
the choicest silver for you.
26 Surely then you will find delight in
the Almighty
and will lift up your face to God.
27 You will pray to him, and he will hear you,
and you will fulfill your vows.
28 What you decide on will be done,
and light will shine on your ways.
29 When people are brought low and you say,
'Lift them up!'
then he will save the downcast.
30 He will deliver even one who is not innocent,

who will be delivered through the cleanness of
your hands."

As you read these verses, do you see this as truth that you
are living out or is it just "head" knowledge? It is key that
we continually submit ourselves to God every moment of every
day. As usual, this is something that is easier said than done. But
wouldn't it be better to submit yourself to God and be at peace
with him? Why spend our time thinking through things and running around in circles when we can submit ourselves to him?

The idea of submitting can be over spiritualized sometimes
and not always clear as to what it looks like to submit to him. It's
really rather simple. Stop. The instructions are clearly written in
these verses. Submit to God. Find peace in him. Accept his instruction. Lay up his words in your heart. There is so much good in
needing the Lord.

DAY 278

Job 23:10-17

10 But he knows the way that I take;

when he has tested me, I will come forth as gold.

11 My feet have closely followed his steps;

I have kept to his way without turning aside.

12 I have not departed from the commands
of his lips;

I have treasured the words of his mouth more
than my daily bread.

13 "But he stands alone, and who can oppose him?

He does whatever he pleases.

14 He carries out his decree against me,

and many such plans he still has in store.

15 That is why I am terrified before him;

when I think of all this, I fear him.

16 God has made my heart faint;

the Almighty has terrified me.

17 Yet I am not silenced by the darkness,

by the thick darkness that covers my face.

God refines and is faithful. Who can oppose God? He does what He pleases!

DAY 279

Job 32:1-13

1 So these three men stopped answering Job, because he was righteous in his own eyes. 2 But Elihu son of Barakel the Buzite, of the family of Ram, became very angry with Job for justifying himself rather than God. 3 He was also angry with the three friends, because they had found no way to refute Job, and yet had condemned him. 4 Now Elihu had waited before speaking to Job because they were older than he. 5 But when he saw that the three men had nothing more to say, his anger was aroused. 6 So Elihu son of Barakel the Buzite said:

"I am young in years,

and you are old;

that is why I was fearful,

not daring to tell you what I know

7 I thought, 'Age should speak;

advanced years should teach wisdom.'

8 But it is the spirit[b] in a person,

the breath of the Almighty, that gives them understanding.

9 It is not only the old[c] who are wise,

not only the aged who understand what is right.

10 "Therefore I say: Listen to me;

I too will tell you what I know.

11 I waited while you spoke,
I listened to your reasoning;
while you were searching for words,
12 I gave you my full attention.
But not one of you has proved Job wrong;
none of you has answered his arguments.
13 Do not say, 'We have found wisdom;
let God, not a man, refute him.'

E lihu is one of those characters in the Bible that stands out. He was wise enough to let the older ones speak first, but also doesn't claim to be smart in his young age because of human wisdom. He knows he is being led by the Holy Spirit of God and that is what is compelling him to speak wisdom to Job and his friends.

There are so many instances in my life where I have prayed and said, "Lord, you want me to do WHAT?!? You want me to say that?!? That's crazy!!!" At the same time, I love being led by the Holy Spirit because he has challenged me to do or say things that I would have never done in my wildest dreams. Allow yourself to take on the challenge of being led by his spirit! Not everything will work out as you may think, but allow your confidence and wisdom to rest in the Lord. Remember that it is all about Him — it's not about you.

Day 280

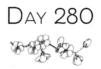

Job 34:33

34 "Men of understanding declare,
   wise men who hear me say to me,
   "Should God then reward you on your terms,
   when you refuse to repent?"

This question that Elihu is led to ask Job and his friends is one that I easily wrestle with in my heart at this time. I wrestle with it because clearly the answer is that the Lord can and will reward me on his terms. How often does the Lord give us opportunities to trust him and then it doesn't work out as we thought it should? We lose hope and get disappointed, rather than waiting on the Lord to reward us on his terms.

Who's to say that the Lord is still working and preparing us for something greater OR that he needs to do some work in the other individual's life to make them ready for a greater reward?

Turn off your "instant microwave" thinking and just wait. Be like a crockpot — the reward is worth it!

DAY 281

Job 36:16

16 "He is wooing you from the jaws of distress
to a spacious place free from restriction,
to the comfort of your table laden with
choice food.

How INCREDIBLE is this verse?!? My brothers and sisters, we have and serve a good God. He is wooing us. He is active. The verb "wooing" is present tense. Is this something that was written to Job in the past to only apply to him? No! God is wooing you today. Right now!

Look at your trials and frustrations in light of this verse. How is God wooing you out of the jaws of distress to a spacious place? If it is too hard to see the answer to that question at this moment, ask God to show you. Remember who Job is to God. Remember what he has been through up until this point.

Our Daddy wants to woo you out of the dark restricted places. For the icing on the cake, he wants to bring you to the comfort of your table laden with choice foods. Feast your eyes on how God is wooing you!

DAY 282

Job 38-40
Chapter 38-40

f you are feeling like all that and a bag of chips, just read Job chapters 38-40 and you will soon feel small in comparison to God!

DAY 283

Job 42:1-3

1 Then Job replied to the Lord:

2 "I know that you can do all things;

no purpose of yours can be thwarted.

3 You asked, 'Who is this that obscures my plans without knowledge?'

Surely I spoke of things I did not understand,

things too wonderful for me to know.

When you look at future plans for your life, do you look at them through the way that Job responds to God?

God can do all things.

No purpose of his can be thwarted.

Have you spoken of plans that you did not understand?

It is so encouraging to know there is a promise of God that tells us that none of his purposes can be thwarted. We may not always have the knowledge of the "why?" or the things too wonderful to know, but have patient endurance. Don't just take time to know of God. Take time to know God and his purposes.

DAY 284

Revelation 20:12

12 And I saw the dead, great and small, standing before the throne, and books were opened. Another book was opened, which is the book of life. The dead were judged according to what they had done as recorded in the books.

As sons or daughters of God, we know that our names are written in the book of life. Yet, there is something so empowering about being able to read this verse out loud. We can claim the promise that our name is written down by the hand of the Almighty! We will stand before the Lord and be judged accordingly based on what is already written down. Does that bring joy or fear into your heart?

Day 285

Jeremiah 31:9-12

9 They will come with weeping;
they will pray as I bring them back.
I will lead them beside streams of water
on a level path where they will not stumble,
because I am Israel's father,
and Ephraim is my firstborn son.
10 "Hear the word of the Lord, you nations;
proclaim it in distant coastlands:
'He who scattered Israel will gather them
and will watch over his flock like a shepherd.'
11 For the Lord will deliver Jacob
and redeem them from the hand of those
stronger than they.
12 They will come and shout for joy on the
heights of Zion;
they will rejoice in the bounty of the Lord—
the grain, the new wine and the olive oil,
the young of the flocks and herds.
They will be like a well-watered garden,
and they will sorrow no more.

How well do you do with waiting on the Lord? Are you open to falling into the arms of His word and allowing him to bring you the comfort you need? Remind yourself daily of the promises throughout His Word. He will deliver you. He will redeem you from the hand of those who are stronger than you. Rejoice in Him! Today, may you face every moment with the expectation of God's deliverance and redemption — and respond with joy and praise!

DAY 286

Jonah 1:2-3

2 "Go to the great city of Nineveh and preach against it, because its wickedness has come up before me."

3 But Jonah ran away from the Lord and headed for Tarshish. He went down to Joppa, where he found a ship bound for that port. After paying the fare, he went aboard and sailed for Tarshish to flee from the Lord.

The word of the Lord came to Jonah very clearly. But, as would be probably many of our responses — if we're being honest, Jonah's was to flee from the Lord. It was a conscious decision that Jonah made to run. If you are in a situation where the Lord is speaking to you and giving you instruction to move forward, but you want to run from Him — then the story of Jonah is definitely for you. Think before you decide to run and remember, the Lord has your best in mind. After all, he is the Creator of the Universe, so he can handle your life.

Day 287

Jonah 1:6

6 The captain went to him and said, "How can you sleep? Get up and call on your god! Maybe he will take notice of us so that we will not perish."

Did you notice that the captain refers to Jonah's "god" with a small g? It shows how limited our human knowledge and our acknowledgement of God can be.

DAY 288

Jonah 1:9

9 He answered, "I am a Hebrew and I worship
the Lord, the God of heaven, who made the sea
and the dry land."

Jonah doesn't have a problem fleeing from the Lord, but then he
so openly acknowledges who the Lord is and that the Lord is
who he worships. A question we must ask ourselves, how often do
we do this same thing in our own lives?

DAY 289

Jonah 1:10

10 This terrified them and they asked, "What have you done?" (They knew he was running away from the Lord, because he had already told them so.)

The sailors were then terrified. They seemed to have some great understanding to know who God was, enough to be terrified. I love what is written in parenthesis of verse 10,

"They knew he was running away from the Lord because he had already told them so."

How does that come up in conversation amongst a bunch of unbelieving sailors? Wouldn't that have been great to have been a fly on the wall during that conversation? Praise God for the random things that are added throughout the Bible stories.

DAY 290

Jonah 1:14-16

14 Then they cried out to the Lord, "Please, Lord, do not let us die for taking this man's life. Do not hold us accountable for killing an innocent man, for you, Lord, have done as you pleased." 15 Then they took Jonah and threw him overboard, and the raging sea grew calm. 16 At this the men greatly feared the Lord, and they offered a sacrifice to the Lord and made vows to him.

The sailors' response is quite drastic as they cry out to Him that they should not die. It makes me wonder what their relationship was with the Lord or was this their first encounter with the Lord? Whatever the answers may be to these questions, their response was such that they feared the Lord. They brought offerings of sacrifice and made vows to the Lord.

What an incredibly intimate time to have been on that ship!

Do you remember your first encounter or acknowledgement of the Lord in your life?

DAY 291

Jonah 2:2
2 He said:
"In my distress I called to the Lord,
and he answered me.
From deep in the realm of the dead I called for help,
and you listened to my cry.

The encouragement for you today is this: God listens to us even when we are "deep in the realm of the dead". If we call to Him, he will hear our cry and help us.

DAY 292

Jonah 2:6

6 To the roots of the mountains I sank down;
the earth beneath barred me in forever.
But you, Lord my God,
brought my life up from the pit.

The last sentence of this verse is such a simple promise to rest in for today. "But, you, Lord my God, brought my life up from the pit." There is always room for the Lord's redemption no matter where we may be in life.

DAY 293

Jonah 2:8
8 "Those who cling to worthless idols
turn away from God's love for them."

Life is so often busier than we may know what to do, which can create many opportunities to cling to worthless idols — turning away from the Lord.

Take a moment to slow down today! His love and the peace that comes is well worth the time!

DAY 294

Jonah 3:8

8 But let people and animals be covered with sackcloth. Let everyone call urgently on God. Let them give up their evil ways and their violence.

Praise the Lord that the Ninevites had a King that pointed them to the Lord Almighty — urgently!

Prayer: Lord, would you provide leaders in my life that would urgently lead me to the Lord. Amen.

DAY 295

Jonah 3:9

9 Who knows? God may yet relent and with compassion turn from his fierce anger so that we will not perish."

It is good to listen to the Lord, to read his Word. To build on yesterday's devotional reading, as we pray for the Lord to provide leaders in our lives that will point us to the Lord, we must also prepare our hearts to listen to what the Lord says to us through those individuals — that we may experience his compassion.

DAY 296

Jonah 3:10

10 When God saw what they did and how they turned from their evil ways, he relented and did not bring on them the destruction he had threatened.

Our walk with the Lord is not just a one time deal of turning to the Lord, only to sit back and watch him do all the work. No, my friend, it is about looking for everything that is good and beautiful — both in the darkness and the light.

Verse 10 is a reminder that our God is truly a compassionate God as we turn from our evil ways. He will relent and not bring on the destruction that we so often deserve.

Today may be full of really hard things, but I encourage you to turn back to the Lord and look for EVERYTHING that is good and beautiful!

DAY 297

Jonah 4:4
4 But the Lord replied, "Is it right for you to be angry?"

This chapter holds such an annoyingly pertinent question for our lives if you are one, like me, who struggles with anger. That's right! Truth be told, I am human in a fallen world which means I need verses like verse 4 that seemingly come out of the blue as I am reading through God's word.

The bluntness of God is so pure and beautiful in this question that he puts before Jonah. Can you hear God's voice in this question as if you were in Jonah's place? To make it even more personal, maybe there is a situation or person you are facing that really angers you. Allow yourself to hear the Lord ask you today, "Is it right for you to be angry?"

This question is a good one to remember for sure!

Day 298

Esther 2:1

1 Later when King Xerxes' fury had subsided, he remembered Vashti and what she had done and what he had decreed about her.

Today's devotional is a reminder and life lesson to learn from his Word! There really is something in the Bible for everything! This is a great example of why you should not make decisions when you are drunk because you may lose your wife.

Day 299

Esther 2:10-11

10 Esther had not revealed her nationality and family background, because Mordecai had forbidden her to do so. 11 Every day he walked back and forth near the courtyard of the harem to find out how Esther was and what was happening to her.

There are so many women in this world that are "forbidden" to do certain things. Yes, sometimes it is for their own protection and other times it is because they are being controlled in a negative way.

No matter what Mordecai's reasoning was for forbidding Esther from sharing her nationality and family background, she chose to obey his word. Let us take a moment to think outside of our own situations — no matter how difficult or joyful they may be — and pray for the many women in this world who are in situations where they are forbidden to have a voice or, even bigger, the freedom to openly follow our loving Heavenly Father. He sees them too, even if they don't feel seen!

DAY 300

Esther 2:12

12 Before a young woman's turn came to go in to King Xerxes, she had to complete twelve months of beauty treatments prescribed for the women, six months with oil of myrrh and six with perfumes and cosmetics.

In order to go in and see the King, the women had to go through 12 months of beauty treatments!

If you are a man reading this devotional, stay with me through the end of this—I promise it is worth it!

For the women reading this, can you imagine someone coming up to you and saying, "You have to go through 12 months of beauty treatments in preparation for a man"? Honestly, I would probably laugh in their face and walk the other way!

We, as single women, can spend so much time trying to make ourselves beautiful based on what we think might make a man satisfied — not even knowing if he will accept us. And, let's face it, rejection can be brutal!

As I grow older, the Lord has shown me the deepening joy of who I am in Him. I don't just say that as a nice "Christian" statement. It is so important that we find our confidence in the Lord and walk in obedience to Him. Speaking from my own experience: When walking in obedience to the Lord toward a relationship, a possible rejection is easier to take hold of because you have the Living God of the Universe to run to!

Now men, I haven't forgotten about you! If you are Prince Charming awaiting your Princess, don't forget to ask the Lord what his expectations are for you to lead a woman well. I can't imagine having to lead a woman or family, but I pray that you all will be brave enough to rise to the occasion! Don't make us go through 12 months of beauty treatments in preparation for you!

DAY 301

Esther 2:17

17 Now the king was attracted to Esther more than to any of the other women, and she won his favor and approval more than any of the other virgins. So he set a royal crown on her head and made her queen instead of Vashti.

The Lord has a plan for each of us. As crazy as a time-frame of waiting and preparation may be, hold fast to the Lord! His timing is perfect and He will bring you favor.

Writing that truth out for others to read in the days and years to come is an easy thing to do. Living it out in my own life — let's just say, I need to read it just as much as the next person. I wouldn't trade that truth for anything. The waiting can be hard. I know that full well. Remember, you can always ask the question of the Lord, "What do you want me to get out of this?"

Just be willing to wait for his response and walk in obedience — even in the silent spaces. He is still working!

Day 302

Esther 3:1-15

1 After these events, King Xerxes honored Haman son of Hammedatha, the Agagite, elevating him and giving him a seat of honor higher than that of all the other nobles. 2 All the royal officials at the king's gate knelt down and paid honor to Haman, for the king had commanded this concerning him. But Mordecai would not kneel down or pay him honor.

3 Then the royal officials at the king's gate asked Mordecai, "Why do you disobey the king's command?" 4 Day after day they spoke to him but he refused to comply. Therefore they told Haman about it to see whether Mordecai's behavior would be tolerated, for he had told them he was a Jew.

5 When Haman saw that Mordecai would not kneel down or pay him honor, he was enraged. 6 Yet having learned who Mordecai's people were, he scorned the idea of killing only Mordecai. Instead Haman looked for a way to destroy all Mordecai's people, the Jews, throughout the whole kingdom of Xerxes.

7 In the twelfth year of King Xerxes, in the first month, the month of Nisan, the pur (that is, the

lot) was cast in the presence of Haman to select a day and month. And the lot fell on[a] the twelfth month, the month of Adar.

8 Then Haman said to King Xerxes, "There is a certain people dispersed among the peoples in all the provinces of your kingdom who keep themselves separate. Their customs are different from those of all other people, and they do not obey the king's laws; it is not in the king's best interest to tolerate them. 9 If it pleases the king, let a decree be issued to destroy them, and I will give ten thousand talents[b] of silver to the king's administrators for the royal treasury."

10 So the king took his signet ring from his finger and gave it to Haman son of Hammedatha, the Agagite, the enemy of the Jews. 11 "Keep the money," the king said to Haman, "and do with the people as you please."

12 Then on the thirteenth day of the first month the royal secretaries were summoned. They wrote out in the script of each province and in the language of each people all Haman's orders to the king's satraps, the governors of the various provinces and the nobles of the various peoples. These were written in the name of King Xerxes himself and sealed with his own ring. 13 Dispatches were sent by couriers to all the king's provinces with the order to destroy, kill and

annihilate all the Jews—young and old, women and children—on a single day, the thirteenth day of the twelfth month, the month of Adar, and to plunder their goods. 14 A copy of the text of the edict was to be issued as law in every province and made known to the people of every nationality so they would be ready for that day.

15 The couriers went out, spurred on by the king's command, and the edict was issued in the citadel of Susa. The king and Haman sat down to drink, but the city of Susa was bewildered.

Today, may our hearts be burdened to pray for the authorities in our lives whether that is a boss, a pastor, a congressman, or even the President of the United States. Yes, we all have our opinions, but as believers, we are called to pray for those in authority. They have a great opportunity to be a voice for good, but our world is crazy.

The King in chapter 3 doesn't seem to have a mind of his own. He just does what people manipulate him to do and in turn, sends out a decree to kill all the Jews.

I urge you to not just pray for the authorities, but also those under them whose job it is to inform them of what is going on in order to help them make a choice. We are all empowered to have a voice. We must be careful in how we influence those around us.

DAY 303

Esther 5:4-5

4 "If it pleases the king," replied Esther, "let the king, together with Haman, come today to a banquet I have prepared for him."
5 "Bring Haman at once," the king said, "so that we may do what Esther asks."

What is the beauty of a King not having a mind of his own? In this situation with Queen Esther going before him, we see the clear evidence that God is going with Queen Esther and giving her much favor. In earlier chapters, the king was just drunk and got mad.

As you read this daily devotional, there is no way of me knowing what you may be going through today. If you are hurting deeply or rejoicing loudly, be reminded that God is faithful and will show you his favor!

Day 304

Esther 5:11-13

11 Haman boasted to them about his vast wealth, his many sons, and all the ways the king had honored him and how he had elevated him above the other nobles and officials. 12 "And that's not all," Haman added. "I'm the only person Queen Esther invited to accompany the king to the banquet she gave. And she has invited me along with the king tomorrow. 13 But all this gives me no satisfaction as long as I see that Jew Mordecai sitting at the king's gate."

"Lord, this passage kills me because I look at my own life and the ways that I have so often been prideful about my work, and yet, had hatred in my heart towards my brother. I am not any different than Haman, am I?"

It is a sobering thought when you take the time to make this passage of scripture personal. Although it is an opportunity for the Lord to reveal where we still need His overwhelming presence, it isn't an easy lesson to learn. It's one thing to point fingers at Haman and say, "He is so prideful and filled with hatred." At the end of the day, the question is this: How many of those fingers need to be pointed back at ourselves?

DAY 305

Esther 7:6-10

6 Esther said, "An adversary and enemy! This vile Haman!"

Then Haman was terrified before the king and queen. 7 The king got up in a rage, left his wine and went out into the palace garden. But Haman, realizing that the king had already decided his fate, stayed behind to beg Queen Esther for his life.

8 Just as the king returned from the palace garden to the banquet hall, Haman was falling on the couch where Esther was reclining.

The king exclaimed, "Will he even molest the queen while she is with me in the house?"

As soon as the word left the king's mouth, they covered Haman's face. 9 Then Harbona, one of the eunuchs attending the king, said, "A pole reaching to a height of fifty cubits[a] stands by Haman's house. He had it set up for Mordecai, who spoke up to help the king."

The king said, "Impale him on it!" 10 So they impaled Haman on the pole he had set up for Mordecai. Then the king's fury subsided.

There are always two sides to every story. We have heard that many times as we walk through this life. We learned from Day 304, that Haman was full of pride and hatred. The story doesn't stop with that detail — that isn't the only reason for his being impaired.

Realizing that the King had already chosen his fate, Haman stayed behind to beg for his life. In his state of despair, he fell on the couch where Queen Esther was reclining just as the King returned to the room. This only brought more rage to the King. It became personal when Haman fell on the couch with Queen Esther (v. 8).

Today, if you are struggling with a difficult situation or you can't see where the Lord is leading, choose humility. Choose to ask the Lord for His wisdom and clarity to see both sides of the story. Also, ask the Lord to make your heart ready to receive whatever He may have to reveal to you. Trust that He will give you all you need in all situations.

DAY 306

Esther 10:3

3 Mordecai the Jew was second in rank to King Xerxes, preeminent among the Jews, and held in high esteem by his many fellow Jews, because he worked for the good of his people and spoke up for the welfare of all the Jews.

A re you willing to take a challenge today? I don't know about you, but as I read this verse, it brings me great joy to know how Mordecai worked for the good of his people!

Can we take the challenge today to be like Mordecai? If you are a leader or a pastor, how can you work for the good of the flock that the Lord has entrusted to you? If you are a parent, how can you work for the good of your children? Are you in the medical field? How can you work for the good of your patients? Are you an administrative assistant? This question applies to you just as well. How can you work for the good of your boss or those they are leading? Do you have siblings? I'm not letting you off the hook that easy! No matter your age, how can you work for the good of your sibling(s)?

Once you walk in this challenge, watch how the Lord puts you in a place of being held in high esteem! You've got this!

DAY 307

Isaiah 41:13
13 For I am the Lord your God
who takes hold of your right hand
and says to you, Do not fear;
I will help you.

saiah 41 is a chapter I could spend days in, pouring over the powerful characteristics of God! It is well worth the time to read this whole chapter, but I want to focus on verse 13. We have the joy and privilege to face this day knowing that the Lord, our God, will take hold of our right hand. We don't have to fear. He will help us!

Do I want direction and confirmation of future planning — big or small? Yes, of course! The real question, in light of verse 13 that I must ask myself on a daily basis is this: Do I desire to grow in my relationship with the Lord more than I desire to have direction and confirmation of future plans?

The Lord takes hold of my hand, your hand, that is how close and intimate he is to each of us as we continue in this journey.

DAY 308

Isaiah 41:14

14 Do not be afraid, you worm Jacob,

little Israel, do not fear,

for I myself will help you," declares the Lord,

your Redeemer, the Holy One of Israel.

As a continuation from Day 307, verse 14 encourages the people of Israel to not be afraid. Who is the Lord? He is my Redeemer. He is your Redeemer. He is Israel's Redeemer. The power and strength of the Lord that we draw from this verse is worth allowing ourselves to deeply breathe in! If that doesn't make you want to stand upon the Rock of Ages and believe in the Living God, I am not sure what will!

Day 309

Jeremiah 15:15-18

15 Lord, you understand;
remember me and care for me.
Avenge me on my persecutors.
You are long-suffering—do not take me away;
think of how I suffer reproach for your sake.
16 When your words came, I ate them;
they were my joy and my heart's delight,
for I bear your name,
Lord God Almighty.
17 I never sat in the company of revelers,
never made merry with them;
I sat alone because your hand was on me
and you had filled me with indignation.
18 Why is my pain unending
and my wound grievous and incurable?
You are to me like a deceptive brook,
like a spring that fails.

Today's passage is rather heavy and a bit depressing to read. If you were looking for a "pick me up" devotional day, these verses probably aren't the ones you want to dwell on! At the same time, it is good and brings great delight that there are passages like this in God's word.

It provides a reminder that when the pain is deep or seems unending, it is okay to sit before the Lord and be blunt with Him. Whatever you have to say in the midst of your pain or lack of understanding, the Lord can take it.

I have walked through such days where the pain was deep. I didn't understand why doors were closing. It hurt. The pain in my heart was filled with hopelessness. No matter the pain, it was still very evident that I could cry out to the Lord and tell him like it is.

He strengthened me. Don't be afraid to look into the Lord's eyes and speak directly. He delights in you and loves you.

Day 310

Jeremiah 15:19-21

19 Therefore this is what the Lord says:

"If you repent, I will restore you

that you may serve me;

if you utter worthy, not worthless, words,

you will be my spokesman.

Let this people turn to you,

but you must not turn to them.

The Lord responds! We learned in previous verses that it is okay to speak directly to the Lord in the midst of our pain. If you have ever been down in the dumps or said ugly words that impede your mind, you know it can be difficult to wait for the Lord's response.

Today, take the command in verse 19 that the Lord gives us to speak "worthy" not "worthless" words. Be the Lord's spokesman and see how your day turns out!

DAY 311

Jeremiah 15:20-21

20 I will make you a wall to this people,
a fortified wall of bronze;
they will fight against you
but will not overcome you,
for I am with you
to rescue and save you,"
declares the Lord.
21 "I will save you from the hands of the wicked
and deliver you from the grasp of the cruel."

In today's devotional, there is a very strong recurring theme that our God is faithful. He will carry us through anything and everything. His character tells us that He is the Redeemer. We just need to practice his presence. The Lord says to repent, so that we may serve Him and our enemies won't overcome us. The Lord promises to rescue and save us! Rest in this promise and let it wash over the deepest parts of your soul!

Day 312

Jeremiah 17:5-6
5 This is what the Lord says:
"Cursed is the one who trusts in man,
who draws strength from mere flesh
and whose heart turns away from the Lord.
6 That person will be like a bush in the wastelands;
they will not see prosperity when it comes.
They will dwell in the parched places of the desert,
in a salt land where no one lives.
A prayer for today:

Dear Heavenly Daddy,
It is a sobering thought to think upon what it really means to have my heart turn away from you because I drew strength from man. In those areas where I have fallen short, would you press into those places and help me to not be a bush in the wasteland?
Cleanse me, oh my Lord. Show me your delight as you pour over me with your love. I am undeserving, but you are greater still.
In Your Name I Pray,
Amen

DAY 313

Jeremiah 17:7-8

7 "But blessed is the one who trusts in the Lord,
whose confidence is in him.
8 They will be like a tree planted by the water
that sends out its roots by the stream.
It does not fear when heat comes;
its leaves are always green.
It has no worries in a year of drought
and never fails to bear fruit."

Most of these devotional thoughts are written from a time in my life where I had been let go from my job. I soon found myself in a place of waiting upon the Lord to remove so many broken areas of my life. I found that I had the joy of the Lord making me raw before him.

In order to determine whether I would return to my job, I was asked to come under another authority as I moved back home. I learned one of the most important lessons the Lord wanted to teach me.

He showed me that I needed to put my confidence in Him and Him alone.

Although God's word says that our authorities will give account for those that are placed under them, we are also called — as individuals — to place our confidence in the Lord.

Prayer: *ABBA. Father. Daddy, would you make me, your child, like a tree planted by the stream? A tree that doesn't fear the heat because I, by your grace, put my confidence in you daily, hourly, minute by minute.*

In Your Strength,

Amen.

DAY 314

Jeremiah 17:9-10

9 The heart is deceitful above all things
and beyond cure.
Who can understand it?
10 "I the Lord search the heart
and examine the mind,
to reward each person according to their conduct,
according to what their deeds deserve."

If we read Jeremiah 17:5-10 as a whole, what it comes down to is putting our confidence in the Lord and trusting Him. He is the One who will search our hearts and examine our minds.

Who am I to judge whether I am good enough to serve or fill a role at any particular place of employment? And who is an authority to decide that? To be honest, I would not want to decide the will of a person without first trusting the Lord and putting my confidence in Him.

Pray without ceasing.

Prayer: *Dear Lord, in light of Jeremiah 17:5-10, would you please grant wisdom and discernment to each of us as we discern your will for ourselves or even for others? May you examine our hearts and our minds as only you know how truly deceptive the heart is. Oh that we would find your reward according to our deeds. Amen.*

Day 315

Jeremiah 18:4-9

4 But the pot he was shaping from the clay was marred in his hands; so the potter formed it into another pot, shaping it as seemed best to him.

5 Then the word of the Lord came to me. 6 He said, "Can I not do with you, Israel, as this potter does?" declares the Lord. "Like clay in the hand of the potter, so are you in my hand, Israel. 7 If at any time I announce that a nation or kingdom is to be uprooted, torn down and destroyed, 8 and if that nation I warned repents of its evil, then I will relent and not inflict on it the disaster I had planned. 9 And if at another time I announce that a nation or kingdom is to be built up and planted,

Remember God is the potter and he has the power to do whatever he thinks is best as we walk in obedience or disobedience to him.

Day 316

Jeremiah 20:7-10

7 You deceived me, Lord, and I was deceived;
you overpowered me and prevailed.
I am ridiculed all day long;
everyone mocks me.
8 Whenever I speak, I cry out
proclaiming violence and destruction.
So the word of the Lord has brought me
insult and reproach all day long.
9 But if I say, "I will not mention his word
or speak anymore in his name,"
his word is in my heart like a fire,
a fire shut up in my bones.
I am weary of holding it in;
indeed, I cannot.
10 I hear many whispering,
"Terror on every side!
Denounce him! Let's denounce him!"
All my friends
are waiting for me to slip, saying,
"Perhaps he will be deceived;
then we will prevail over him
and take our revenge on him."

t would seem that Jeremiah is having a bit of a pity party in front of the Lord. He complains that all he does is prophesy violence and destruction. That doesn't sound like a fun role to be in. People are mocking him. His friends are against him.

He is open with the Lord, though he doesn't hesitate to complain or wrestle with the fact that he knows he is doing what the Lord has asked of him. If Jeremiah does not get the Lord's message out, then it burns like a fire within him. He grows weary.

Do you ever feel like that? Do you ever just want to tell the Lord how hard life is, even though you know you are doing what he has asked you to do? Be comforted. Jeremiah gets it. Do not grow weary. Patient endurance, my friend.

DAY 317

Jeremiah 20:11

11 But the Lord is with me like a mighty warrior;
so my persecutors will stumble and not prevail.
They will fail and be thoroughly disgraced;
their dishonor will never be forgotten.

D id you notice how much hope and reassurance is in this verse? If you are faithful to the Lord's direction in your life, as well as, to do what he says, the Lord will be with you. He will be with you like a mighty warrior. The persecutors will not prevail. Praise the Lord!

DAY 318

Jeremiah 20:12-13

12 Lord Almighty, you who examine the righteous
and probe the heart and mind,
let me see your vengeance on them,
for to you I have committed my cause.
13 Sing to the Lord!
Give praise to the Lord!
He rescues the life of the needy
from the hands of the wicked.

Abba Father, Daddy! Oh that we would crawl up on your lap, drawing strength and increasingly deep knowledge from the presence of your word today!

Our God is real and active. He examines the righteous. He probes our hearts and minds. The vengeance is all His to claim and do with what he desires. Sing to the Lord! Praise Him!

Even though verse 13 was written thousands of years ago, it is still in present tense which means it is as prevalent for us to practice today as it was in Jeremiah's time. So, whatever your cause may be, his word actively and presently tells us that he rescues the life of the needy. Present your cause and wait upon him with praise and expectancy!

DAY 319

Jeremiah 21:10
10 I have determined to do this city harm and not good, declares the Lord. It will be given into the hands of the king of Babylon, and he will destroy it with fire.'

The wrath of God is real! Yet, this is never really talked about in church. God's wrath is evident to Jeremiah. It is all in the context of people who disobeyed.

God determined to do harm, not good, to the city because of their disobedience.

We talk so much about God's grace and how we must give one another grace. Are we aware of the reality of his wrath? Are we willing to walk in obedience to God? And if we aren't, are we willing to experience his wrath?

DAY 320

Jeremiah 23:16
16 This is what the Lord Almighty says:
"Do not listen to what the prophets are prophesying to you;
they fill you with false hopes.
They speak visions from their own minds,
not from the mouth of the Lord.
It's always more powerful to read the Bible in
context. Don't ever take that for granted.

Verse 16 holds a great piece of advice straight from the mouth of the Lord. He tells us not to listen to the prophets because they are filling us with false hopes as they speak. They tell of visions from their own minds, not from the mouth of the Lord.

As I look at this verse, I can't help but see how this somewhat describes how easy it is to think out loud when advising someone. This is not to say that the advice we think out loud is necessarily wrong, but we should be careful in what thoughts come out. Those thoughts may be louder than we realize.

Are we speaking from the mouth of the Lord or our own mind?

DAY 321

Jeremiah 23:17-18

17 They keep saying to those who despise me,
'The Lord says: You will have peace.'
And to all who follow the stubbornness of
their hearts
they say, 'No harm will come to you.'
18 But which of them has stood in the council
of the Lord
to see or to hear his word?
Who has listened and heard his word?

These verses bring a directness that we should not easily walk away from. We should run to the Lord and see His Word, praying for those who prophesy lies.

If you are in any place of leadership, it is important to be careful in what you say to the people the Lord has placed under you. Although there is no perfect leader; they are all human. It really drives me to pray for our leaders in the church as they take on the roles they have been entrusted with — no matter how new or old that role may be.

Prayer:

Lord, I pray that our church leaders would not give false hope or think out loud, but that they would stand in Your presence in every moment. May they continuously grow in humility.

Amen

A few questions to consider and ask yourself as you go through your day:

1. Am I seeking to see and hear the word of the Lord?

2. Am I being judgmental and speaking from my mind?

3. What am I hearing from the Lord about a specific situation that I am currently praying about?

DAY 322

Jeremiah 23:19-20
19 See, the storm of the Lord
will burst out in wrath,
a whirlwind swirling down
on the heads of the wicked.
20 The anger of the Lord will not turn back
until he fully accomplishes
the purposes of his heart.
In days to come
you will understand it clearly.

S eriously! If you question God's authority or power, well, question no more!

Thank you, God, for the proof that your wrath is for real. Amen.

This brings so much wisdom and knowledge of God's character if we choose to walk in disobedience to Him.

Day 323

Jeremiah 23:21-22

21 I did not send these prophets,
yet they have run with their message;
I did not speak to them,
yet they have prophesied.
22 But if they had stood in my council,
they would have proclaimed my words
to my people
and would have turned them from their evil ways
and from their evil deeds.

Have you ever noticed how easy it is to tack on the words, "and the Lord said", to any statement as if we were speaking straight from the mouth of the Lord?

Together, these two verses paint a picture of our continuous need to be one on one in the presence of God's counsel. What it comes down to is putting your confidence in what God is speaking through people.

I am thankful to have people that speak into my life, I am even more thankful for the Lord teaching me the lesson that it is more important to run to him than to man! It is better to be one who runs to the Lord and stands in his counsel than to be a people pleaser. Don't shut out those who the Lord has directed you to, but be willing to test their words with what the Lord is speaking to you! That is more honoring to them and the Lord than anything else.

Day 324

Jeremiah 23:23-24
23 "Am I only a God nearby,"
declares the Lord,
"and not a God far away?
24 Who can hide in secret places
so that I cannot see them?"
declares the Lord.
"Do not I fill heaven and earth?"
declares the Lord.

Even in His wrath, His word is still flawless! Turn each of these simple questions from the Lord into promises:

1. "Am I only a God nearby and not a God far away?"

Promise: God is nearby, he is never far away.

2. "Who can hide in secret places so that I cannot see them?"

Promise: God can see you always. You cannot hide from him.

3. "Do not I fill heaven and earth?"

Promise: Our God is a big God who fills the heavens and the earth.

DAY 325

Jeremiah 23:36

36 But you must not mention 'a message from the Lord' again, because each one's word becomes their own message. So you distort the words of the living God, the Lord Almighty, our God.

We are not to say, "This is a message from the Lord", because it just becomes our own message and we distort the words of the Living God, the Lord Almighty. Can you imagine? In other words, make sure you take time to sit in His counsel if you are going to speak His message.

Day 326

Jeremiah 24:4-7

4 Then the word of the Lord came to me: 5 "This is what the Lord, the God of Israel, says: 'Like these good figs, I regard as good the exiles from Judah, whom I sent away from this place to the land of the Babylonians. 6 My eyes will watch over them for their good, and I will bring them back to this land. I will build them up and not tear them down; I will plant them and not uproot them. 7 I will give them a heart to know me, that I am the Lord. They will be my people, and I will be their God, for they will return to me with all their heart.

The promises the Lord declares over his people:

1. He calls us the good fig.

2. There will be times that he sends us into exile.

3. His eyes will watch over us for our good.

4. He will bring us back to "this land".

5. He will build us up and not tear us down.

6. He will plant us and not uproot us.

7. He will give us a heart to know Him as the Lord.

8. We will be his people and he will be our God.

9. We will return to Him with all of our heart.

10. No matter whether He has us in exile or plants us in the land, He is always with us. He provides stability!

These 10 promises stand true for us today, just as they did thousands of years ago! Talk about legit stability!

Day 327

Jeremiah 32:39-41

39 I will give them singleness of heart and action, so that they will always fear me and that all will then go well for them and for their children after them. 40 I will make an everlasting covenant with them: I will never stop doing good to them, and I will inspire them to fear me, so that they will never turn away from me. 41 I will rejoice in doing them good and will assuredly plant them in this land with all my heart and soul.

This promise that God says he will give his people, "singleness of heart and action, so that they will always fear me", is an incredible promise for a people who He brought out of Egypt into the Promised Land. And yet, they still walked in disobedience.

God's love for his people is evident as we continue to read verses 40-41. He speaks of inspiring them to fear him. Oh to be inspired to fear the Lord Almighty! How awesome and powerful our God is! He is a personal God even when he is talking about the masses.

Allow God to silence your heart in this moment and ask him how you might pray this passage of scripture over the many lost souls in this world that have yet to hear His Name. Maybe there is a specific country or city that you want to pray for at this time.

My prayer is this: *God, would you please inspire the believer and unbeliever to fear you so they will not turn away from you, but that they would have a singleness of heart and action? And, Daddy, would you please teach me how to pray this promise over myself and walk it out in belief and faith? In Your Name I Pray, Amen.*

Day 328

Jeremiah 39:17-18

17 But I will rescue you on that day, declares the Lord; you will not be given into the hands of those you fear. 18 I will save you; you will not fall by the sword but will escape with your life, because you trust in me, declares the Lord.'"

There was so much gore in Jerusalem as it was being taken over. There was room for fear and terror and darkness. But God. God brings this intimate promise, telling them how He is going to rescue them and they no longer have to fear, because they trusted Him.

Every one of us can easily pinpoint something that we fear. If we want to get real personal and real with ourselves, there are many things we fear. Our fear may be the fear of spiders or sharks. Or it could be the fear of getting some illness or being alone with no one to care for you. These are all very real fears.

I, personally, can quickly relate to the fear of being alone with no one to care for me. Now, I can actively choose to live in that fear and assume the worst, that I will never get married or have someone to care for me solely as I lose my sight. But, the Lord is gracious. The Lord loves me deeply enough to put verses 17-18 of Jeremiah, chapter 39, in the Bible so that I would have something to apply to such a fear.

Every single one of us can take these verses and know that the Lord will not give us into the "hands" of whatever we may fear. He will save us. We can escape with our life because we have trusted in the Lord. He knows our fears and our weaknesses. The reality is, we can trust Him and he declares that over us!

Day 329

Jeremiah 42:1-6

1 Then all the army officers, including Johanan son of Kareah and Jezaniah[a] son of Hoshaiah, and all the people from the least to the greatest approached 2 Jeremiah the prophet and said to him, "Please hear our petition and pray to the Lord your God for this entire remnant. For as you now see, though we were once many, now only a few are left. 3 Pray that the Lord your God will tell us where we should go and what we should do."

4 "I have heard you," replied Jeremiah the prophet. "I will certainly pray to the Lord your God as you have requested; I will tell you everything the Lord says and will keep nothing back from you." 5 Then they said to Jeremiah, "May the Lord be a true and faithful witness against us if we do not act in accordance with everything the Lord your God sends you to tell us. 6 Whether it is favorable or unfavorable, we will obey the Lord our God, to whom we are sending you, so that it will go well with us, for we will obey the Lord our God."

A lthough I am only emphasizing Jeremiah 42:1-6, the bigger picture lies in the context of chapters 42-43. These chapters are filled with a play by play scenario of God's direction for the people, and yet, the people think they know better. It is helpful to know that there is a place in scripture that sheds light on the whole concept of asking someone to pray for you and advise you on what God says.

Questions to ask ourselves:

1. Why, so often, do we think we know better than the Lord?

2. Why do we ask someone to pray and speak on behalf of God if we are not going to walk in obedience to the Lord?

3. An even bigger question, how often have you or I been in such a scenario as this in our own lives?

It is good to know that the Bible is filled with so many disobedient people who say they will obey and then they turn their backs on Him. Someday we will be in perfect, all consuming glory with God.

Walk in obedience to what God tells you and look forward with anticipation to His glory!

Day 330

Jeremiah 44:15-26

15 Then all the men who knew that their wives were burning incense to other gods, along with all the women who were present—a large assembly—and all the people living in Lower and Upper Egypt, said to Jeremiah, 16 "We will not listen to the message you have spoken to us in the name of the Lord! 17 We will certainly do everything we said we would: We will burn incense to the Queen of Heaven and will pour out drink offerings to her just as we and our ancestors, our kings and our officials did in the towns of Judah and in the streets of Jerusalem. At that time we had plenty of food and were well off and suffered no harm. 18 But ever since we stopped burning incense to the Queen of Heaven and pouring out drink offerings to her, we have had nothing and have been perishing by sword and famine."

19 The women added, "When we burned incense to the Queen of Heaven and poured out drink offerings to her, did not our husbands know that we were making cakes impressed with her image and pouring out drink offerings to her?"

20 Then Jeremiah said to all the people, both men and women, who were answering him, 21 "Did not the Lord remember and call to mind the incense burned in the towns of Judah and the streets of Jerusalem by you and your ancestors, your kings and your officials and the people of the land? 22 When the Lord could no longer endure your wicked actions and the detestable things you did, your land became a curse and a desolate waste without inhabitants, as it is today. 23 Because you have burned incense and have sinned against the Lord and have not obeyed him or followed his law or his decrees or his stipulations, this disaster has come upon you, as you now see."

24 Then Jeremiah said to all the people, including the women, "Hear the word of the Lord, all you people of Judah in Egypt. 25 This is what the Lord Almighty, the God of Israel, says: You and your wives have done what you said you would do when you promised, 'We will certainly carry out the vows we made to burn incense and pour out drink offerings to the Queen of Heaven.'

"Go ahead then, do what you promised! Keep your vows! 26 But hear the word of the Lord, all you Jews living in Egypt: 'I swear by my great name,' says the Lord, 'that no one from Judah living anywhere in Egypt will ever again invoke my name or swear, "As surely as the Sovereign LORD lives."

In chapter 44, the message is clear that they should go ahead and do whatever they were going to do anyways, but there are consequences. We can learn from these two chapters whether we are a child or an adult. Are you open and willing to walk in obedience to whatever the Lord might be wanting to say to you today?

DAY 331

Ezekiel 13:22-23

22 Because you disheartened the righteous with your lies, when I had brought them no grief, and because you encouraged the wicked not to turn from their evil ways and so save their lives, 23 therefore you will no longer see false visions or practice divination. I will save my people from your hands. And then you will know that I am the Lord.'"

A new day brings new insight to this passage! God will save us from false visions and lies, then the wicked will know that He is God. Praise the Lord for this word of truth!

Day 332

Ezekiel 22:30-32

30 "I looked for someone among them who would build up the wall and stand before me in the gap on behalf of the land so I would not have to destroy it, but I found no one. 31 So I will pour out my wrath on them and consume them with my fiery anger, bringing down on their own heads all they have done, declares the Sovereign Lord."

Did your heart hit the floor as you read verse 30? It is such a depressing verse unless you understand who the Lord was searching among. The Israelites were so rebellious, it explains so much of why the Lord could not find anyone to stand in the gap on behalf of the land.

The Lord searched and found noone. He chose to pour out his wrath upon them based on what they had done. Oh how sin can overtake us if we allow it. Even so, we know who the Lord is in all of this as verse 32 ends with, "declares the Sovereign Lord".

Day 333

Ezekiel 43:1-3

1 Then the man brought me to the gate facing east, 2 and I saw the glory of the God of Israel coming from the east. His voice was like the roar of rushing waters, and the land was radiant with his glory. 3 The vision I saw was like the vision I had seen when he came to destroy the city and like the visions I had seen by the Kebar River, and I fell facedown.

Think about if you were in Ezekial's place, seeing the glory of the Lord right before you! I imagine that hearing the voice of the Lord, "the rushing waters", would be like standing in front of Niagara Falls. That is what Ezekiel was experiencing!

The verse goes on to say that the "land was radiant with his glory". It is hard to wrap my mind around what all this would be like.

Reminder for the day: Be face down before the Lord.

What if you took on that posture for today? Maybe you can't physically be face down, but how do we mentally walk through today, face down before the Lord?

Day 334

Ezekiel 43:4-5

4 The glory of the Lord entered the temple through the gate facing east. 5 Then the Spirit lifted me up and brought me into the inner court, and the glory of the Lord filled the temple.

Verse 5 speaks for itself! Talk about having the fear of the Lord, being lifted up and brought into the inner court. Can you even begin to imagine the intimacy of our God in this?

What would it mean or look like to live our lives in such a way that we are continuously in awe of God — to be face down before the Lord – no matter what the current circumstance may be? What would it mean to walk through each day in anticipation of meeting the Lord in the inner court?

Prayer: *God, would you please help me to be in awe of the little things you have done in my life? I get so focused on what isn't happening and then I am not "face down" in prayer or in fear of you. I am sorry for my lack of faith in you. Amen.*

The Word is your battle plan!

DAY 335

Daniel 1:4

4 young men without any physical defect,
handsome, showing aptitude for every kind of
learning, well informed, quick to understand,
and qualified to serve in the king's palace. He
was to teach them the language and literature of
the Babylonians.

I s there such a man out there that fits all these standards? These
seem to be awfully high standards, but they're a great place to
start as you pray for your future spouse.

This can be applied in many different situations:

1. If you have already found your spouse, take time today to
   pray for the Lord to enable your spouse to be steadfast in
   these characteristics.

2. If you have unmarried children or grandchildren, ask the
   Lord what he would have you pray for in a spouse for them.

3. Take it one step further, think of someone in your church
   or local area, and pray for them by name, that their spouse
   would be raised up to be a Godly man or woman — not
   based on your standards, but on God's.

DAY 336

Daniel 1:6-7

6 Among those who were chosen were some from Judah: Daniel, Hananiah, Mishael and Azariah. 7 The chief official gave them new names: to Daniel, the name Belteshazzar; to Hananiah, Shadrach; to Mishael, Meshach; and to Azariah, Abednego.

If you have grown up in the church, you have been taught the story of "Daniel in the Lions Den" and "Shadrach, Meshach, and Abednego in the Fiery Furnace". Because these stories are often taught separately, I never realized that these four guys were chosen and went through name changes at the same time. With this knowledge, it makes their stories that much stronger in light of the work of the hand of God.

We all have our individual stories that the Lord is writing for us on our behalf as he works in our lives. But, take a moment, and think about your family members, friends, or even your co-workers — what about their story has had an impact on your life? Then flip that question around, what in your own story has had an impact in others' lives?

God created us to work together. To be a community of sorts. Imperfect and a work in progress. That we may glorify His Name as we live this life he has entrusted to us!

Day 337

Daniel 1:8

8 But Daniel resolved not to defile himself with the royal food and wine, and he asked the chief official for permission not to defile himself this way.

Verse 8 is a great example of having to stand up for your beliefs. It is a good thing to have your own opinions or voice in a certain situation you are facing. But, what is your attitude? Where is your heart and mind as you speak? Is it that of just wanting to be heard and be right? Or is it filled with humility, compassion, and expectation that the Lord will give you favor?

DAY 338

Daniel 1:9

9 Now God had caused the official to show favor
and compassion to Daniel,

In verse 9 it says, "Now God caused the official to show favor and compassion to Daniel". What do you even do with a statement such as this? Yes, Daniel stepped out and spoke up, so the focus could very easily be placed on Daniel. Him speaking up, though, could have also ended very badly.

The response, instead, puts the focus on God. "Now God caused" — our focus should be God and God alone.

How is God bringing you favor and compassion through the authorities around you?

DAY 339

Daniel 1:10

10 but the official told Daniel, "I am afraid of my lord the king, who has assigned your food and drink. Why should he see you looking worse than the other young men your age? The king would then have my head because of you."

D id you notice how full of honesty the official is about his fears towards his lord, the king? What an awesome view of the grace of God. I highly doubt that this conversation between Daniel and the official would have happened if the Lord wasn't present.

Remember that our leaders, authorities, moms, and dads are all human. They feel fear too. They will, one day, have to give an account before the Lord.

DAY 340

Daniel 1:11-12

11 Daniel then said to the guard whom the chief official had appointed over Daniel, Hananiah, Mishael and Azariah, 12 "Please test your servants for ten days: Give us nothing but vegetables to eat and water to drink.

D aniel becomes the spokesman and "drags" the other three into the test. How do you think the three guys felt about eating only veggies and drinking water for 10 days? Daniel is bold and stepped out in faith!

If someone came up to you and said, "You can only eat veggies and drink water for the next 10 days." I think my initial response would be, "I hope they are well seasoned veggies and taste really good!"

How do you think you would respond?

Day 341

Daniel 1:13-14

13 Then compare our appearance with that of the young men who eat the royal food, and treat your servants in accordance with what you see." 14 So he agreed to this and tested them for ten days.

I t seems like a fair plan that is proposed in verse 13. What a way to step out in faith and trust God!
Some questions that come to mind:

1. Were there any doubts in their minds like, "Okay, God, are you really going to come through?"

2. Did they just have holy confidence in the Sovereign Lord?

3. What did all four of these guys experience in those 10 days of testing?

4. What were their emotions?

5. What did they experience in their physical bodies?

6. What were their prayer times like in between meals and at meals?

Although we may not have the answers to these questions, we can still implement them into our own lives and situations of testing. It may not be food that the Lord is calling you to give up as a way of testing, but whatever it is, are you willing to seek the Lord to find ways to grow closer to him?

DAY 342

Daniel 1:15-16

15 At the end of the ten days they looked healthier and better nourished than any of the young men who ate the royal food. 16 So the guard took away their choice food and the wine they were to drink and gave them vegetables instead.

P raise the Lord! He came through for these four men! Have hope in what you sense is from the Lord. He will carry you through!

Hold fast to the Lord – even when the outcome isn't what you expect. He is not a God of confusion.

Day 343

Daniel 1:17

17 To these four young men God gave knowledge and understanding of all kinds of literature and learning. And Daniel could understand visions and dreams of all kinds.

This story in these last several devotional days has not just been about the Lord showing himself mighty in a single way in the lives of these four men, but rather, his mightiness is reigning true on several different levels! As the men stepped out in faith and went through the test, the Lord brought them good health. The story doesn't stop with the perks of a good diet.

Our Sovereign Lord takes it so much further, giving each of these men knowledge and understanding of all kinds of literature and learning.

So, my friend, would you say it is worth it to endure the testing knowing that the Lord will meet you on multiple different levels — physically, mentally, and spiritually? Even in the deepest, lowest, hardest point of testing, are you anticipating how the Lord will come through for you? Remember, our Heavenly Daddy sees you even in your darkest hour.

Day 344

Daniel 2:27-30

27 Daniel replied, "No wise man, enchanter, magician or diviner can explain to the king the mystery he has asked about, 28 but there is a God in heaven who reveals mysteries. He has shown King Nebuchadnezzar what will happen in days to come. Your dream and the visions that passed through your mind as you were lying in bed are these:

29 "As Your Majesty was lying there, your mind turned to things to come, and the revealer of mysteries showed you what is going to happen. 30 As for me, this mystery has been revealed to me, not because I have greater wisdom than anyone else alive, but so that Your Majesty may know the interpretation and that you may understand what went through your mind.

There is no one on the human level who can explain the dream the king had. Initially, that sounds so hopeless to be told there is no one that can interpret your dream or relate to what you are going through. Talk about feeling alone!

There are always two sides to every story, right? Daniel goes on to proclaim truth by explaining that there is a God in heaven that is the Revealer of Mysteries. What a relief! No offense to my fellow man, but I would much rather trust in the God of Heaven, who is the Creator of the Universe, to solve my problems. Knowing there is a Revealer of Mysteries is so freeing because it takes the weight off of my shoulders to solve all the problems.

In verse 29, it says that the King's mind turned to things to come. Being an Enneagram 6 (personality), my mind is always focused on things to come or creating worse case scenarios. Our God is not one who just leaves us to figure out our dreams on our own. He shows us what is to come.

Daniel could have completely taken credit for having the knowledge to be able to reveal that journey. Instead, he gives all the credit to the Revealer of Mysteries. The dream wasn't revealed to Daniel because he had greater wisdom than anyone else alive. It was revealed to him so that the king may know and understand what was going to happen.

Oh God, You do not withhold any good thing. You give wisdom and understanding! If you are stumped on a problem at work, in your personal life, or maybe you have a friend that is struggling with something you are helping them through — the encouragement here would be to turn it over to the Revealer of Mysteries and wait upon Him. He's got this! And He's got you!

DAY 345

Daniel 3:15

15 Now when you hear the sound of the horn,
flute, zither, lyre, harp, pipe and all kinds of
music, if you are ready to fall down and worship
the image I made, very good. But if you do not
worship it, you will be thrown immediately into
a blazing furnace. Then what god will be able to
rescue you from my hand?"

Can you say, "conceited"? It is interesting that he uses a lower-case "g" for "God". It goes to show how small our minds can be in the knowledge it contains when we aren't focused on God. Of course, none of the man-made gods can save them — they are inanimate objects who are completely powerless.

When you create a god, whether that is TV or music or a relationship, aren't you the one who gives it power over you?

There is no god that can rescue you from your hand, King Nebi! Especially if you have created any of them! No one created God. He has been around since the beginning of time. He is God and there is no other. End of story.

Day 346

Daniel 3:16-17

16 Shadrach, Meshach and Abednego replied to him, "King Nebuchadnezzar, we do not need to defend ourselves before you in this matter. 17 If we are thrown into the blazing furnace, the God we serve is able to deliver us from it, and he will deliver us[a] from Your Majesty's hand.

Amen! The Lord is our Defender! He WILL deliver us and is more than able. These verses bring such a strong, bold and faith-filled message. What a great example of how to verbally throw down Satan and claim the power of God!

Walk tall today with your head lifted high in this truth that the Lord is your Defender. See how differently your day turns out.

Day 347

Daniel 3:18

18 But even if he does not, we want you to know, Your Majesty, that we will not serve your gods or worship the image of gold you have set up."

What does one even say about such a verse as this since it speaks for itself? We often ask ourselves, "What if?" But, did you ever think to change that question into a statement and say, "Even if..."? Even if God does not come through. Even if we die. Even if.

Even in the midst of them standing up for what they believe, they were still respectful to the King and called him, "Your Majesty". In other words they are saying, "With all due respect, we won't bow down." What a way to go out!

Day 348

Daniel 3:24-27

24 Then King Nebuchadnezzar leaped to his feet in amazement and asked his advisers, "Weren't there three men that we tied up and threw into the fire?"

They replied, "Certainly, Your Majesty."

25 He said, "Look! I see four men walking around in the fire, unbound and unharmed, and the fourth looks like a son of the gods."

26 Nebuchadnezzar then approached the opening of the blazing furnace and shouted, "Shadrach, Meshach and Abednego, servants of the Most High God, come out! Come here!"

So Shadrach, Meshach and Abednego came out of the fire, 27 and the satraps, prefects, governors and royal advisers crowded around them. They saw that the fire had not harmed their bodies, nor was a hair of their heads singed; their robes were not scorched, and there was no smell of fire on them.

This passage brings some humor to mind. It is a very serious and disturbing situation in regards to humans being burned alive, simply because they wouldn't do what their "authority" wanted them to do. But, what strikes humor is verse 25, which says, "He said, 'Look, I see four men walking around in the fire, unbound and unharmed, and the fourth looks like a son of the gods.'"

If you were in such a situation where you were walking around in the fiery furnace with God, what do you think would be going through your mind? What would that have felt like to be surrounded by fire and not get burned?

Day 349

Daniel 5:3-6

3 So they brought in the gold goblets that had been taken from the temple of God in Jerusalem, and the king and his nobles, his wives and his concubines drank from them. 4 As they drank the wine, they praised the gods of gold and silver, of bronze, iron, wood and stone.

5 Suddenly the fingers of a human hand appeared and wrote on the plaster of the wall, near the lampstand in the royal palace. The king watched the hand as it wrote. 6 His face turned pale and he was so frightened that his legs became weak and his knees were knocking.

Drinking out of the cups from the temple of God and then praising gods of gold and silver, is clearly not a good move on their part. They are just begging God to make a statement! God did just that as the human hand appeared and began writing on the wall! Verse 5 so descriptively portrays the fingers appearing and where in the palace the writing on the wall took place. It brings such a vivid picture, as if you are standing in the room with the King.

Our God is real, no doubt about that. When you hear of a situation like this, what is your response? Does it feel normal to hear that a hand would appear and begin writing on the wall? Or do you feel a response like the King had, where his knees were knocking? Do we fear the Lord and His Sovereignty? Or are we afraid of the Lord?

There are a lot of questions in that last paragraph, but I hope that you will take time today to think through them, knowing that the expectation isn't to come up with all the answers right here and right now. Be patient with yourself and whatever the Lord may want to teach you.

Day 350

Daniel 6:14

14 When the king heard this, he was greatly distressed; he was determined to rescue Daniel and made every effort until sundown to save him.

I t goes to show that no human being or person of authority can save us. As we are obedient to the Lord — we will face "Lion's Den" experiences. It is almost like Daniel got thrown under the bus. He went against the decree of the King, but obviously those who opposed Daniel forgot the "writing on the wall" experience King Darius had a chapter before this.

Man cannot save us, but God can. He is the God of justice and we should never mess with his servants.

DAY 351

Daniel 6:16

16 So the king gave the order, and they brought Daniel and threw him into the lions' den. The king said to Daniel, "May your God, whom you serve continually, rescue you!"

It boggles my mind how the King doesn't favor Daniel and throws him into the Lion's Den, but points to God to save him. Not just to save him one time. No! He uses the word, "continually".

Working in a ministry, it is easy to acknowledge that there is a God who saves. It is good to be reminded that not everyone works in ministry or a church. Many of you who are reading this have been given a "mission field" of a secular workplace — where it may not even be OK to acknowledge God with those you work with or the authorities you come in contact with. If you are in a secular job situation, I would encourage you to pray that the Lord would be present and acknowledge Him — only He knows what that is going to look like in your given situation. Don't be afraid to take ownership of your faith and pray that others will acknowledge Him to save you continuously, even if they don't know Him. Look for everything good and beautiful.

Day 352

Hosea 2:13
13 I will punish her for the days
she burned incense to the Baals;
she decked herself with rings and jewelry,
and went after her lovers,
but me she forgot,"
declares the Lord.

I was not prepared to read the sadness and beauty of this chapter. God is intimate and full of compassion. There are some really key verses to hold tight to, especially if you — like me — struggle with feeling worthless in light of things from your past.

Verse 13 is one of the most depressing verses in the Bible. Whether you are a prostitute or have lowered yourself to that lack of worth by other standards — in one way or another, we have all chased after our "lovers" and have forgotten the Lord. This is a humbling reality.

Day 353

Hosea 2:14
14 "Therefore I am now going to allure her;
I will lead her into the wilderness
and speak tenderly to her.

No matter what your day brings or what your past may hold, we have and serve a God who longs to speak tenderly, even though we may have forgotten Him.

Praise the Lord! THAT'S how much He loves us! If you are feeling dirty or worthless — God Almighty, the One true and Living God — is waiting to allure you and me into the wilderness, one on one.

Do you know how loved you are by God?

Why do we turn from our First Love?

Are you willing, today, to be allured by God into the wilderness to have some one-on-one time with Him?

Day 354

Hosea 2:15
15 There I will give her back her vineyards,
and will make the Valley of Achor a door of hope.
There she will respond as in the days of her youth,
as in the day she came up out of Egypt.

The Lord restores. He makes each of us, his children, a door of hope. On our good days when we want to praise the Lord because everything is going well with our soul, seize that door of hope. If it is dark for you today, it may not be easy, but allow surrender. The Lord will restore. He wants to show you everything that is good and beautiful. He wants to give back to you, to me. Will we allow him this pleasure?

It's okay to praise Him, even on the dark days.

DAY 355

Hosea 2:16
16 "In that day," declares the Lord,
"you will call me 'my husband';
you will no longer call me 'my master.'

God is my husband. God is your husband. Can you imagine having a human love you the way that God does? How does a man lead his wife as unto the Lord? And if he is doing so, then does that make the wife love and worship the Lord — her true husband — more?

I think about the time in my life that the Lord asked me to seriously seek Him about having a relationship with someone. In those times of praying for God's leading, I experienced a deeper sense of praise and worship towards God. I am not even sure how to put it into words. There was a strong sense of being loved by a man based on God's word and his deep relationship with God.

There was a lack of knowledge in knowing how to be a.good girlfriend and, eventually — Lord willing — a good Godly wife, who would stand alongside him in whatever God called him to do. Even though there was that lack of knowledge, I knew that God would be the one leading this future love every step of the way.

Whether you are currently single or married, it is so incredibly important that we look to God to be our First Love, our Husband, who will lead; otherwise loneliness or unmet expectations will take over.

Day 356

Hosea 2:19-20

19 I will betroth you to me forever;
I will betroth you in righteousness and justice,
in love and compassion.
20 I will betroth you in faithfulness,
and you will acknowledge the Lord.

To define the word betrothed is to say it is the person to whom you are engaged or pledged to be married to.

These two verses sound like a really good deal. They are incredible, all-encompassing promises to hold on to. When you read verses such as these, how can you walk away and not want a relationship with the LORD?

Embrace your betrothed.

DAY 357

Hosea 3:1-5

1 The Lord said to me, "Go, show your love to your wife again, though she is loved by another man and is an adulteress. Love her as the Lord loves the Israelites, though they turn to other gods and love the sacred raisin cakes."

2 So I bought her for fifteen shekels[a] of silver and about a homer and a lethek[b] of barley. 3 Then I told her, "You are to live with me many days; you must not be a prostitute or be intimate with any man, and I will behave the same way toward you."

4 For the Israelites will live many days without king or prince, without sacrifice or sacred stones, without ephod or household gods. 5 Afterward the Israelites will return and seek the Lord their God and David their king. They will come trembling to the Lord and to his blessings in the last days.

The LORD restores Hosea and his wife to one another. Can you imagine having a lover of other men or other things, but then having your husband buy you back? It's interesting that Hosea never fights the Lord on this one — talk about things being unfair and needing to forgive, even though mistakes were made!

God loves us no matter what we have done!

Day 358

Hosea 6:1-3

1 "Come, let us return to the Lord.
He has torn us to pieces
but he will heal us;
he has injured us
but he will bind up our wounds.
2 After two days he will revive us;
on the third day he will restore us,
that we may live in his presence.
3 Let us acknowledge the Lord;
let us press on to acknowledge him.
As surely as the sun rises,
he will appear;
he will come to us like the winter rains,
like the spring rains that water the earth."
Healing.

The Lord brings healing to our pain and our wounds. Can you even begin to comprehend the overwhelming power of what it means to drink in His ability to break and heal us?

Prayer: *Lord, thank you for this beautiful passage of scripture. How do I even begin to take it all in? Amen.*

Stop. Allow your heart and mind to be silenced and dwell on that healing before you read further.

Ready?

Verse two is a prophecy of what was to come with Jesus' death on the cross. The Lord restores Jesus on the third day. Are you open to praying in faith for healing in three days for whatever you may be going through? It's not a matter of whether the Lord CAN bring healing in three days, but rather do we have the faith to believe Him?

It is okay to not be okay. It is okay to not be there yet with the faith to believe. But read on to verse three.

"Let us press on to acknowledge him..." This is something I, personally, need to speak over myself time and time again.

DAY 359

Hosea 7:13
13 Woe to them,
because they have strayed from me!
Destruction to them,
because they have rebelled against me!
I long to redeem them
but they speak about me falsely.

Throughout Christian history, many have turned away from the Lord and by coming against Christian ministries. At the time that I originally came across this verse in my daily reading, there was an email that hit my inbox speaking negatively about a missions organization. Hosea is a book filled with the Lord's redemption. The Lord longs to redeem us. The question is, are we willing?

It becomes more and more apparent how much I, myself, need to repent and work on forgiveness towards others — as long as I am in the human body and living on this earth — forgiveness will be an ongoing process.

Through forgiveness, I will be kept from growing bitter and landing myself in a group that is against a ministry or those that are doing the Lord's work so faithfully.

Prayer: *Dear Lord, Thank you that you long to redeem those who have spoken against you. There is also that reality and truth that you will bring destruction to them.*

In those areas of my own life where I have sinned or spoken against you — would You continually call me to a place of surrender and redemption? Amen.

DAY 360

Hosea 7:15

15 I trained them and strengthened their arms,
but they plot evil against me.

This is such a simple, but loaded, verse. In light of eternity with our Savior who died on the cross for our sins — there are no words. It would be easy to point fingers at others who are against Christian work. Wait. We must also look in the mirror and ask ourselves, "How many times has the Lord trained me and strengthened my arms, only for me to plot evil against him?"

That question is a hard one to swallow, let alone to answer.
Listen for His voice and act accordingly.

DAY 361

Hosea 12:6

6 But you must return to your God;
maintain love and justice,
and wait for your God always.

This verse! It makes me smile so much and want to imprint it on my forehead as a reminder of how I am to walk through this life — both in the easy and the dark periods of life. It holds so much tenderness and, yet again, it is another verse that sums it all up.

"...wait for your God always."

Day 362

Hosea 14:9

9 Who is wise? Let them realize these things.
Who is discerning? Let them understand.
The ways of the Lord are right;
the righteous walk in them,
but the rebellious stumble in them.

Have you ever had those moments when you are having your daily time with the Lord and then He allows that piece of scripture to play out somewhere in your day? Well, that is what this verse represents to me. I can't remember the context of the conversation I was having with a friend, but the Lord allowed me to use this verse as a word of encouragement as we talked.

Do you think you are wise? Do you think you are discerning? It is evident that the Lord has worked mightily throughout my life as he speaks to me and guides me. There are days, though, that I have to wonder if I am wise or discerning. When I begin to doubt or become prideful in my thinking that my ways are greater...that is a good sign that I should stop and refocus.

The second half of verse nine says, "The ways of the Lord are right; the righteous walk in them, but the rebellious stumble in them."

Day 363

Joel 2:12-13
12 "Even now," declares the Lord,
"return to me with all your heart,
    with fasting and weeping and mourning."
13 Rend your heart
    and not your garments.
Return to the Lord your God,
    for he is gracious and compassionate,
    slow to anger and abounding in love,
    and he relents from sending calamity.

The Lord your God. He is gracious. He is compassionate. He is slow to anger. He is abounding in love. So, return to the Lord your God. Enjoy his many characteristics from which He wants to pour so abundantly upon you, His Betrothed!

Day 364

Amos 5:7-8

7 There are those who turn justice into bitterness
and cast righteousness to the ground.
8 He who made the Pleiades and Orion,
who turns midnight into dawn
and darkens day into night,
who calls for the waters of the sea
and pours them out over the face of the land—
the Lord is his name.

These two verses speak for themselves in many ways.
I have watched men and women turn justice into bitterness.
They cast the righteous to the ground.

But here's the deal. You and I serve a God who turns night
into day. He then turns light of day back into the dark of night.
He pours the waters out over the land.

I am not sure what to say about these two verses ... but they
are beautiful!

Our God is much more powerful than we can ever comprehend!

Day 365

Colossians 1:23

23 if you continue in your faith, established and
firm, and do not move from the hope held out
in the gospel. This is the gospel that you heard
and that has been proclaimed to every creature
under heaven, and of which I, Paul, have become
a servant.

Everything Good and Beautiful. As I was nearing the writing
of this devotional day, a friend encouraged me to ask the Lord
the question, "Lord, what are you wanting to teach me as I finish
this project?" Rather instantly as I finished speaking this question
to the Lord, he spoke His answer ever so clearly!

"Be stable and steadfast. Finish out with Colossians 1:23." The
Lord is so direct!

You are almost to the end. As you, too, finish this journey we
have been on together and move on with your life — remember
what it says in Colossians 1:23. Be established and steadfast, not
shifting in the gospel you heard. We are given stewardship to make
his Word known — his Word, the mystery hidden for ages, but
now being revealed to his Saints!

Although this devotional has been written from much of my
experience as I walked through a tough period in my life, what
you have learned as you have worked your way through each

day, is between you and the Lord. My experiences, yes. But it's not about me.

He is the Great I AM. He is compassionate. He is slow to anger. He is your Betrothed. Be stable in your faith and take His Gospel forth, my friend! Share the "Good and Beautiful" with those around you!

I leave you with what Paul writes in Colossians 1:25-26:

25 I have become its servant by the commission God gave me to present to you the word of God in its fullness— 26 the mystery that has been kept hidden for ages and generations, but is now disclosed to the Lord's people.

CPSIA information can be obtained
at www.ICGtesting.com
Printed in the USA
LVHW012205031022
729859LV00014B/518